A MISSION TO THE MEDIEVAL MIDDLE EAST

A MISSION TO THE MEDIEVAL MIDDLE EAST

THE TRAVELS OF BERTRANDON DE LA BROQUIÈRE TO JERUSALEM AND CONSTANTINOPLE

BY

BERTRANDON DE LA BROQUIÈRE

TRANSLATED BY
THOMAS JOHNES

INTRODUCTION BY

MORRIS ROSSABI

I.B. TAURIS
LONDON · NEW YORK · OXFORD · NEW DELHI · SYDNEY

I.B. TAURIS
Bloomsbury Publishing Plc
50 Bedford Square, London, WC1B 3DP, UK
1385 Broadway, New York, NY 10018, USA

BLOOMSBURY, I.B. TAURIS and the I.B. Tauris logo
are trademarks of Bloomsbury Publishing Plc

First published in Great Britain in 1807 as The Travels of Bertrandon de la Brocquière

First published by I.B. Tauris & Co. Ltd in 2019
Paperback edition first published 2021

Introduction © Morris Rossabi, 2019
Morris Rossabi has asserted his right under the Copyright,
Designs and Patents Act, 1988, to be identified as Author of the Introduction.

All rights reserved. No part of this publication may be reproduced or
transmitted in any form or by any means, electronic or mechanical,
including photocopying, recording, or any information storage or retrieval
system, without prior permission in writing from the publishers.

Bloomsbury Publishing Plc does not have any control over, or responsibility for,
any third-party websites referred to or in this book. All internet addresses given
in this book were correct at the time of going to press. The author and publisher
regret any inconvenience caused if addresses have changed or sites have
ceased to exist, but can accept no responsibility for any such changes.

A catalogue record for this book is available from the British Library.

A catalog record for this book is available from the Library of Congress.

ISBN: HB: 978-1-7807-6432-0
PB: 978-0-7556-3849-9
ePDF: 978-1-8386-0795-1
eBook: 978-1-8386-0794-4

To find out more about our authors and books visit
www.bloomsbury.com and sign up for our newsletters.

CONTENTS

Introduction by Morris Rossabi   vii

A Preliminary Discourse   1
The Second Part   44
The Travels of la Broquière   83

INTRODUCTION
Morris Rossabi

The Mongolian, and later the Ottoman, expansion of the thirteenth through fifteenth centuries set the stage for Bertrandon de la Broquière's travels in 1432–1433. The empire that the Mongolians conquered in the thirteenth century stretched from Korea to Russia in the north and from south China to Syria in the south, and their incursions into Poland and Hungary witnessed the first direct relationship between Europe and East Asia. Peace eventually prevailed, allowing European and Middle Eastern merchants, missionaries, scientists, engineers, and craftsmen to travel to Central Asia and China. The arrival of the Ottoman Turks, first in West Asia and then in Turkey, in the late fourteenth century, ushered in a period of conflict with the Byzantine Empire and Southeastern Europe. Ottoman control of Palestine and the Holy Lands, which the various crusades had not succeeded in wresting from the Muslim states, was of concern to some Western Europeans. Although most Western European states were preoccupied with their own economic growth, with conflicts among themselves, with their drive towards political unity, and with their relationship to the Pope and the Christian Church, a few sought to explore the possibility of recapturing the Holy Lands. It was in this context that Bertrandon de la Broquière set forth on his official travels to the Ottoman domains.

Yet it was also in the context of an extraordinary number of travellers around the fifteenth-century world. Zheng He (1371–1433), a Chinese eunuch, led one of the largest flotillas in world history on seven sea voyages to Southeast Asia, India, West Asia, and even the east coast of Africa. His last trip in 1432 coincided with Bertrandon de la Broquière's travels. Ruy González de Clavijo (d. 1412), an envoy of Henry III of Castile, reached and stayed in the court of Tamerlane from 1403 to 1405, while Tamerlane's son, Shāh Rukh, dispatched Ghiyāth al-Dīn Naqqāsh on a memorable journey from Samarkand to Beijing from 1419 to 1421. All three of these voyages produced invaluable accounts of the regions through which the envoys travelled.[1] They often included descriptions of the customs, products, and political organization of foreign areas, as well as the routes taken by the travellers, but the rulers sent the envoys primarily to gather intelligence, mostly about the military of possible adversaries. Bertrandon de la Broquière's account fits that description.

Little is known of Bertrandon's life and career other than the evidence we can glean from his own travel account. Here again, he resembles most of the renowned travellers of the past. Most of our knowledge of Marco Polo, perhaps the most famous traveller in world history, derives from the account that he provided to a writer named Rustichello, who set down his words. Similarly, the report of Rabban Sauma, the first man from China to reach Europe, yields the only information we have about his life and career. By virtue of their spiritual calling, the Jesuits – who journeyed to Asia, the Americas, and other regions and wrote descriptions of the lands to which they had been assigned – reveal little about their own backgrounds. Bertrandon is even more laconic about his childhood and life, but his attitudes and values emerge in his writings.

Philip the III (the Good, 1396–1467, see Figure 1), the Duke of Burgundy, selected Bertrandon as his envoy. Philip had played a pivotal role in Franco–English relations. The Hundred Years' War, which centred on English claims to territory in France, appeared to end with the victory of King Henry V over the French at Agincourt in 1415. At this point, Joan of Arc appeared and claimed that God had chosen her to lead the French armies. Her visions impressed some in the French hierarchy, who persuaded the French king to name her as a monarch. Her forces won some improbable victories but her greatest triumph entailed lifting the spirit of the French. The country's forces began successfully to resist the English, but Joan herself was captured in 1430 by the Burgundians, who at the time were England's allies. Sold to the English by Philip III, she was tried, found to be a 'witch,' and burned at the stake. Yet her inspiration prompted the French to mount significant campaigns, and eventually Philip III, seeking to end the chaos, signed the Treaty of Arras in 1435, recognized Charles II as the French King, and joined the French side for a time. Faced with an almost unified France, England was no longer a formidable foe and thus virtually ended its efforts to have a substantive base on the Continent.

At the same time, Philip III had grandiose dreams, most improbably to be considered the equal of the French King. To bolster his position, he occupied Luxembourg, Holland, Zeeland, and Friesland, among other regions. He also attempted to boost his prestige by producing a spectacular court life: court festivities were lavish, and Philip supported and was a patron of beautiful illustrated manuscripts, tapestries, jewellery, architecture, and music. But what better way to impress Christians than to succeed in routing the Muslims who controlled the Holy Lands, a principal objective for Europeans for more than three centuries. Although it cannot be ruled out that he may have sought a diplomatic resolution of the Ottoman threat, nonetheless he had a personal issue: the Ottoman Turks had captured his father in battle in 1396. He may have wished to avenge his father's inglorious campaign. Before an attempt to challenge the Ottomans could be made, however, he needed reconnaissance about the new Islamic power to the east, and Philip chose Bertrandon to travel to, and provide a first-hand account of, the new rulers of the Holy Land.

Bertrandon's principal assignment was to offer a report on the Ottoman Turks, the last in a line of peoples who had migrated westward from Central Asia, including the Huns and the Seljuk Turks who had weakened and almost destroyed the Byzantine Empire.[2] The Ottomans had begun to prosper with the accession to power of Osman I (r. 1280–1304), who united them. Details about their history were scarce, and Europeans added somewhat to the confusion by calling them 'Ottomans', based upon a misreading of Osman's name. In any event, Osman started the seemingly inexorable drive to dominate all of Anatolia and to overwhelm the declining Byzantine Empire. His descendants, Orhan (r. 1324–1359) and Murat I (r. 1360–1389), first occupied lands to the north towards the Black Sea and southward to the Sea of Marmara. They skirted the Byzantine capital of Constantinople and moved into Bulgaria and Macedonia. As they annexed additional territory, they changed from nomadic conquerors to regular rulers, with specific taxes and principles of land ownership. They received considerable assistance from non-Turks, partly because of their generally tolerant policies towards Jews and Christians. The Jews were a decided minority compared to the Christians, but the Ottomans often employed them as physicians, weavers, and merchants. After the initial conversion of the Hagia Sophia Church into a mosque, which antagonized Christians, the Ottomans developed such policies of accommodation as permission to worship, opportunities for advancement, and support for merchants and artisans for a time, and quelled much Christian discontent.

Bertrandon fails to mention the Duke's reasons for selecting him as a voyager to the Ottoman domains. Was he knowledgeable about military matters? Did he know a variety of foreign languages? Was he chosen because he was a discrete and a consummate diplomat? Had he been abroad at an earlier time? These tantalizing questions cannot be answered. In any event, his account reveals that he was a perceptive observer and a hardy traveller who could overcome the dangers of the journey. Whatever the reasons for his selection, he turned out to be a good choice and carried out his task intelligently and with dispatch.

Born around 1400, Bertrandon set forth on his travels when he was in his early 30s. Until then, he appears to have led a relatively uneventful life as a proprietor of a small fief in Aquitaine. One of his principal responsibilities was supervision of carving and distribution of meats at banquets. He departed on his pilgrimage in February of 1432 and headed south. Was he accompanied by others in his initial travels? He fails to mention many vital details, but he does reveal that he required guides to escort him through the mountain passes separating France from Italy. He rapidly recounts his route to Rome, via Turin, to Florence, and to Spoleto. His account yields no description of these cities except for Rome, which impresses him due to the Christian relics. He continues, in peremptory fashion, to list the cities through Europe to Jaffa. He passes through Venice, the beautiful 'producer of glass ... and wisely governed', and Zara, with the body of St. Simeon, to Crete, with its excellent sailors, to Cyprus and finally to Jaffa. He provides no new information or insights on any of these cities. Thus far, his descriptions do not match the accounts of other great travellers of the past. The Duke of Burgundy, his patron, sought information about the Holy Land and the impediments – including perils on land and sea – to regaining control over these sites and territories. Information about other places was peripheral.

When Bertrandon reaches the Holy Land, his concise and limited descriptions change to more informed and detailed analyses. Although his assignment entailed strategic considerations, he becomes, as a Christian, an avid sightseer. He visits many of the most revered and renowned religious sites, such as the birthplaces of Jesus and of John the Baptist. Although he is impressed with the religious monuments, he notes that Jerusalem 'is a fine large city which looks as if it has seen better days'.[3]

Traveling in areas without a guide book, and perhaps with the most rudimentary maps, Bertrandon was highly dependent on local inhabitants, which often meant he was dependent on the Arab and Muslim populations. The Muslims with whom he occasionally travelled allegedly protected him and saved his life. An Arab escort nursed him through a high fever while he journeyed through the desert. His most faithful companion was a Mamluk Turk who repeatedly assisted him. The Mamluk dynasty had arisen in the thirteenth century, defeated the Ayyubid dynasty, and ruled Egypt and parts of Syria until the Ottomans defeated them in 1513. In 1260 their leader, Qutuz, had routed a Mongolian detachment at the battle of Ayn Jālūt and prevented any further incursions westward by the Mongolian armies. Bertrandon's Mamluk companion literally saved his life. Two Turks they encounter on their travels, tempted by Bertrandon's apparent affluence, suggest to his Mamluk escort that they rob and kill the European. The Mamluk responds that they have all eaten together and that murdering Bertrandon would defy God's wishes. He also cares for Bertrandon during a bout of illness in a mountain crossing, teaches him to shoot a bow and arrow while riding a horse, and negotiates for food and drink during part of Bertrandon's journey. Bertrandon writes that the Mamluk would not accept any payment for his services.

Europeans he encountered en route also assisted him. Genoese merchants whom he met in Bursa (the Ottomans' capital from 1335 to 1363 and still an administrative, religious, and commercial centre), accompanied him to the city of Pera (which they governed), located on the European side of Constantinople, and which is now known as the district of Beyoğlu in

Istanbul. Here he met Jews and Orthodox Christians who lived permanently in the city and who were mostly merchants. In this multi-ethnic and multi-religious city, he also encountered men from Naples and Milan, an indication that the Italian city states continued to navigate the Mediterranean for trade. His most fortuitous encounter was with an Ambassador from Milan, who permitted Bertrandon to join him on a trek to the Ottoman sultan Murad's (r. 1421–1444 and 1446–1451) court. Bertrandon was able to attend and observe an audience with the Sultan, and he describes the formal etiquette, as well as the actual participants in the ceremonies, in great detail. He also points out that no foreigner seeking an audience with the Sultan arrives without gifts. Even as far away as Damascus, Bertrandon came across French, Venetian, Florentine, and Catalan merchants, attesting to the scale of commerce between Europe and the Islamic world.

Yet, as a foreigner, Bertrandon still faced hazards. He frequently appears in disguise, wearing clothing similar to that of the local inhabitants in order to avoid discovery. Disguises also permit him to enter mosques, to visit other sacred sites, and indeed had helped him to reach the old Ottoman capital at Bursa. Moreover, cash was the only acceptable currency on his travels, and carrying so much money made him vulnerable. He could not take off his clothing for fear of robbery or even, perhaps, murder. He repeatedly mentions the abject condition of Christian slaves, and he witnesses a slave auction in which a young, almost naked black girl of fifteen or sixteen years of age is exhibited and sold. Slaves castrated by the Ottomans were another group that he found piteous. During the several occasions when he barely escaped arrest, he must have feared enslavement.

Bertrandon had definite views about the various peoples he encountered. He was ambivalent about Jews. On the one hand, he praises them for their services as interpreters and their intellect; on the other hand, he accepts the story that they stoned a statue of Jesus, which then bled. He is not enthusiastic about Hungarians, writing about one that he did not keep his word, 'like most Hungarians'. The various ambassadors and merchants from the Italian city states repeatedly assist him and allow him access to people and places he wants to meet or to observe. Orthodox Christians appear mostly in a negative light in his work. He found them to be less trustworthy than Turks, who did not share his religion. Traveling through Eastern Europe and the Byzantine Empire, he sees many orthodox churches, but only Hagia Sophia in Constantinople rivets him and merits a lengthy description. His distaste for orthodoxy stemmed from a long history of enmity between Eastern and Western Christianity. Yet Bertrandon praises the Byzantine Empress for her beauty and athleticism.

The Islamic world does receive his praise on occasion, although he recognizes that hostilities with the Muslim world could erupt at any time. Yet he was impressed with some Muslims' generous and charitable nature in inviting the poor to dine with them. As Bertrandon notes, he would have been hungry and cold and would have suffered much more than he did without his Mamluk companion. He was surely surprised that the Ottoman sultan knew of Paris and could speak Italian. The rituals, the etiquette, and the sophistication of the Ottoman court are similarly impressive. He recounts, with awe, a few of the exploits of Temür (or Tamerlane), who had died almost three decades before his travels, but who was still well known in the Middle East and in the Christian world.

Nonetheless, Bertrandon criticizes some of the Islamic world's activities. He notes their hypocrisy in drinking wine, which was forbidden in their religious texts, and he reveals that Muslims, on several occasions, plead with him to sneak liquor to them. He appears to portray another incident in a negative light, perhaps a bizarre act from his perspective, stating that 'Some people ... had seen the place where Muhammad lies, put out their eyes, saying that they cannot and do not want ever to see anything of greater worth'.[4] Even more disturbing are the gruesome executions employed by the Ottoman sultan: 'Advis was flayed, his head cut off, and three others were killed with him. It was a great shame. The head was stuffed with straw and taken to the Grand Turk [the Sultan]'.[5]

Bertrandon's mission, however, entailed a duty to return with a report on the Sultan and on the Ottomans' military capabilities. He had an opportunity to observe the Sultan and describes him as a man who loves hunting and hawking, as well as drinking. When the Sultan is inebriated, he offers lavish gifts to all around him. He allegedly had 300 wives and 25–30 young boys to satisfy his sexual urges. More important, he can rapidly raise an army, and his troops consist not only of his own people but also of Greeks, Macedonians, Albanians, and Serbs. What makes them a potent military force is their discipline and their orderliness. Naturally, like many peoples who were originally nomadic pastoralists, they have a fine cavalry and are skilled with the bow and arrow. They also wear armour and have access to good intelligence. Bertrandon then offers a catalogue of their weapons and strategy, which had intimidated and compelled the Byzantine Empire to pay them tribute.

Despite the Ottomans' vaunted military exploits, Bertrandon opines: 'I don't think, however, for a well-disciplined people, it would be very hard to break and defeat them, given their lack of arms'.[6] By this he meant the Ottomans' relatively inadequate weaponry. He asserts that if Europeans were to pay their troops properly and provide them with adequate supplies, they would overwhelm the Turks. They would need only light armour because of the weakness of the Ottoman arrows. The Europeans also have the advantage of cannon, which could, among other devastating effects, rattle the Ottoman horses and cause them to retreat in disorder. Deliberate setting of fires would also frighten the horses.

Bertrandon's predictions proved to be poor harbingers of the future. The Ottoman sultan Mehmed (r. 1451–1481) showed that Bertrandon was wrong, when he destroyed the Byzantine Empire and occupied its capital of Constantinople in 1453. Bertrandon, who died on 9 May 1459, eventually became aware that his prognostications were erroneous.

However, much of Bertrandon's report offered useful information to Europeans about the regions he visited. For example, he brought attention to a variety of foods, including caviar (which did not appeal to him), as well as yoghurt and flat bread, and he detailed the process of baking flat bread. He describes such other practices or institutions as bazaars and the caravanserais and the role of qadis (or judges). His report also informed the Duke of Burgundy about dominant groups in the areas through which he voyaged, noting, for instance, Venetian domination in commerce with Constantinople. Most striking was the number of European merchants, mostly from the Italian city states, he encountered on his travels. The scale of European trade was substantial.

Although Bertrandon writes mostly about his own observations, he mentions, on occasion, hearsay as fact. He was told about a group of 30,000 women 'in the mountains of Armenia on the Persian frontier'.[7] These 'Amazons' were warriors, but Bertrandon supplies no other details about them. It strains credulity that such a large contingent would not be mentioned in other contemporary sources. Bertrandon's most incredible account is repetition of the legends concerning Prester John, a Christian monarch in the non-Christian world.[8] He claims that Prester John commanded an army of 4 million men and was always preceded by the Cross whenever he travelled. The legend of a Christian ruler in Asia stemmed from an earlier time but was invigorated in the twelfth and thirteenth centuries, with reports of a Nestorian Christian ruler, specifically in Central Asia. The Mongolian invaders of the thirteenth century and their ensuing interactions with Europe contributed to this myth. In fact, several prominent Mongolian women, including Khubilai Khan's mother and his sister-in-law, were Nestorians, and the travel account of Rabban Sauma, a Nestorian who travelled from Beijing to Baghdad in the 1270s, attests to Nestorian communities all along the Silk Roads.[9] Yet no specific Nestorian monarch could be identified as Prester John. Finally recognizing that Prester John was nowhere to be found in Asia, Europeans turned their attention to Ethiopia, where Christianity had taken hold. They would, on occasion, attribute the rise of Christianity to Prester John, a view that influenced Bertrandon.

Bertrandon de la Broquière's report added to Europe's knowledge of the Islamic world, especially about the Ottoman Turks. To be sure, European merchants and ambassadors had reached Byzantium, and a few had even had audiences with the Ottoman sultan and had travelled in the lands newly under Ottoman domination in West Asia and Eastern Europe. They no doubt offered oral descriptions of their travels and their views of these lands, but Bertrandon de la Broquière was unique in presenting a written report.

Also unusual was his portrait of the Ottoman military, offering insights about its weaponry and tactics to his patron, the Duke of Burgundy, even if he turned out to be inaccurate in his assessment of the Ottoman Turks' power and clearly had not foreseen their ability to conquer Byzantium. In his defence, a united Europe might well have staved off the Ottoman invasions. In any event, Bertrandon de la Broquière gave to posterity a fascinating and valuable account of a pivotal period in world history.

Notes

1. The account of the Zheng He mission is translated in J.V.G. Mills, *Ying-yai Sheng-lan: The Overall Survey of the Ocean's Shores*. Cambridge: Cambridge University Press, 1970; a translation of the Clavijo mission is found in Clements Markham, trans., *Narrative of the Embassy of Ruy Gonzalez de Clavijo to the Court of Timour at Samarkand, A.D. 1403–1406*. London: Hakluyt Society, 1859; and a translation of the account of Ming China is K. M. Maitra, *A Persian Embassy to China, being an Extract from Zubdatu't Tawarikh of Hafiz Abru*. New York: Paragon Books Reprint Corporation, 1970.
2. For his report, see Ch. Schefer, *Le Voyage d'Outremer de Bertrandon de la Broquière*. Paris: Ernest Leroux, 1892 among other translations; The best modern translation is by Galen Kline, *The Voyage d'Outremer by Bertrandon de la Broquière*. New York: Peter Lang, 1988; and a useful summary of Bertrandon's significance is Albrecht Classen, ed., *East Meets West in the Middle Ages and Early Modern Times*. Berlin: Walter de Gruyter, 2013, pp. 49–57.
3. Galen Kline, trans., *The Voyage d'Outremer by Bertrandon de la Broquière*. New York: Peter Lang, p. 10.
4. Kline, p. 33.
5. Kline, p. 126.
6. Kline, p. 145.
7. Kline, p. 50.
8. For a brief notice concerning Prester John, see Peter Jackson, *The Mongols and the West, 1221–1410*. London: Pearson Longman, 2005, pp. 20–21 and 97–99. Bertrandon may have received his information about Prester John from the popular, fourteenth-century work of John Mandeville's travels. See Ian Higgins, *The Book of John Mandeville with Related Texts*. Indianapolis: Hackett, 2011. I am grateful to Professor Sarah Covington of Queens College of the City University for this suggestion.
9. Morris Rossabi, 'Khubilai Khan and the Women in his Family', in W. Bauer, ed., *Sino-Mongolica: Festschrift für Herbert Franke*. Wiesbaden: Franz Steiner Verlag, 1979, pp. 153–180; and Morris Rossabi, *Voyager from Xanadu: Rabban Sauma and the First Journey from China to Europe*. New York: Kodansha, 1992; paperback edition Berkeley: University of California Press, 2010.

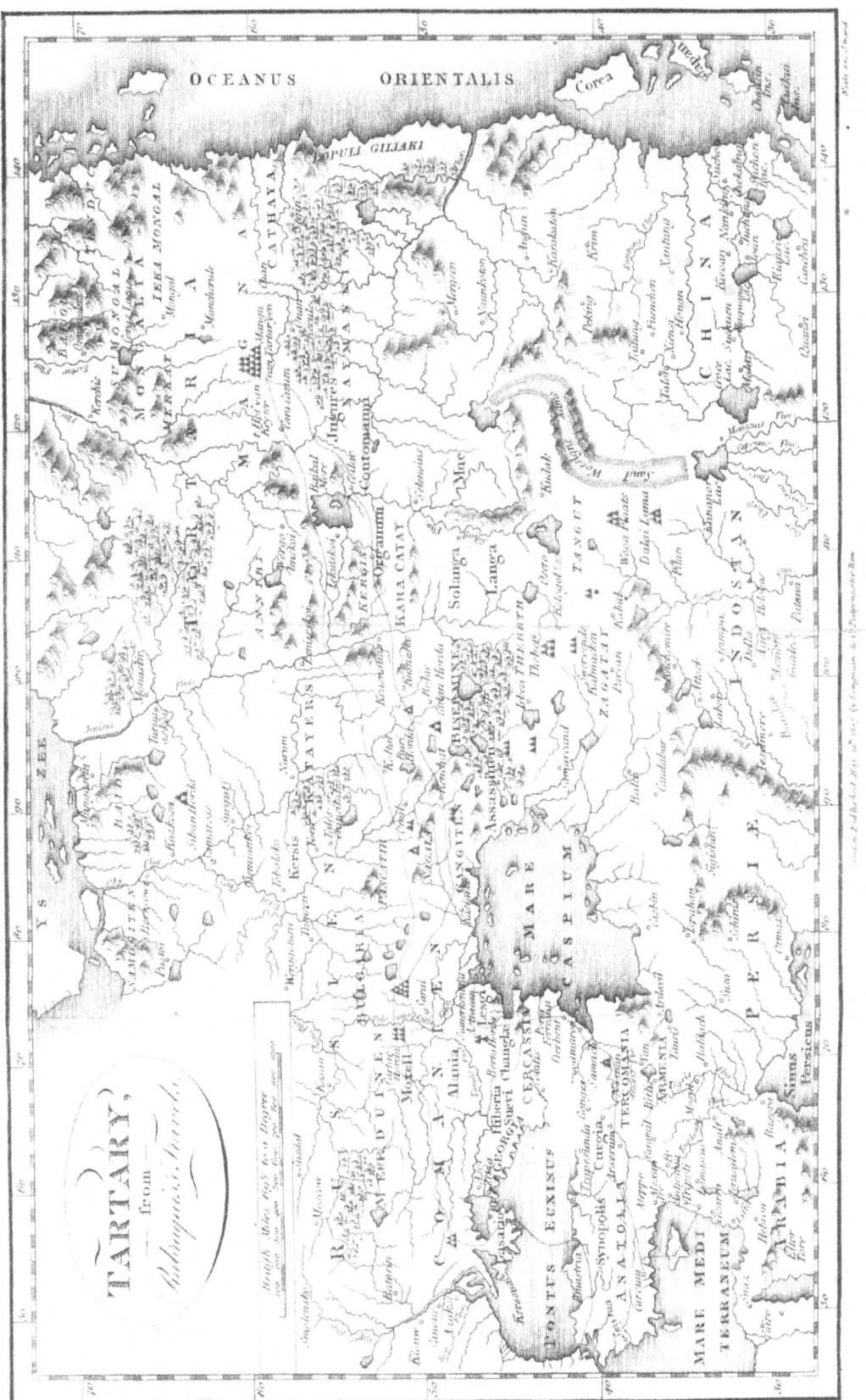

A

PRELIMINARY DISCOURSE..

Accounts of travels published by the French have a very early origin. At the beginning of the fifth century, Rutilius Claudius Numatianus published one, which has been handed down to us incomplete, because death perhaps did not allow him to finish it. The object of his travels was his return from Rome to his own country of Gaul; but as he came by sea, he could only describe the ports and harbours on the coast, and thence has necessarily resulted a monotony in his work, which a man of more genius would have surmounted. Besides, he wished to write a poem, which forced him to assume a poetical tone, and to give poetical descriptions, or such as were so called. In fine, this poem is in the elegiac measure; and every one knows that this kind of versification, the property of which is to interest the idea every two verses, and to confine these verses to a perpetual return of an uniform cadence, is perhaps of all others the least suited to description. When the imagination has much to paint, when at every moment it has need of varied and brilliant pictures, it requires great freedom to display with advantage all its riches: it cannot, therefore, consequently accommodate itself to a double confinement, the infallible effect of which would be to extinguish its fire.

A pagan in religion, Rutilius has shewn his aversion to the Christian doctrine in verses, where, confounding Christians and Jews, he speaks ill of both sects.

It is in consequence of the same sentiments that, having seen on his voyage some monks in the island of Capraia, he wrote against monks the following verses, which I shall quote to give my readers an idea of his style.

> Squalet lucifugis insula plena viris.
> Ipsi se monachos, graio cognomine, dieunt,
>   Quod, soli, nullo vivere teste, volunt.
> Munera Fortunæ metuunt, dum damna verentur:
>   Quisquam sponte miser, ne miser esse queat.
> Quænam perversi rabies tam crebra cerebri,
>   Dum mala formides, nec bona posse pati?'

His work contains curious details in geography, and even some for the antiquary and historian; such, for instance, as his description of a saltmarsh, and the anecdote of the burning of the books of the Sybils at Rome by order of Stilico. There are also some good verses, and among them this in particular on a ruined town:

> ' Cernimus exemplis oppida posse mori.'

But his composition is bad: his descriptions are dry and cold, and his manner pitiful and mean;—no genius, no imagination, and consequently no invention in the pictures he attempts to paint.

Such is his work, at least so it has appeared to me; and it is probably on account of these defects that his poem has been called by the degrading name of ' Itinerary,' under which it is known. There is a french translation of it by le Franc de Pompignan *.

About 505, Arculfus, a bishop of Gaul, made a pilgrimage to Jerusalem. On his return, he wished to publish an account of it, and employed a scots abbot, called Adamanus, to arrange his manuscript notes and his own verbal account. The relation composed by Adamanus, entitled ' De Locis Sanctis,' and divided into three books, was first printed by Gretser, and afterward more completely by Mabillon. Arculfus, having visited the holy land, embarked for Alexandria, thence he crossed over to the island of Cyprus, and

* In the Melanges de Litter. et Poésie, &c. par l'Acad. de Montauban, p. 81.

from Cyprus he went to Constantinople, whence he returned to France.

Such travels certainly promise a great deal; and the man who had to describe Palestine, Egypt, and the capital of the eastern empire, might assuredly have made an interesting work. But the execution of so vast a design required philosophy and knowledge, in which his age was miserably deficient. It is a pilgrimage, and not travels, that the prelate has published. He neither makes us acquainted with the laws, manners, and usages of the people, nor with any thing that concerns the places or countries he passes through, but solely the relics and objects of devotion that were revered there.

Thus, in his first book, which treats of Jerusalem, he tells us of the column to which JESUS was tied when he was scourged,—of the lance that pierced his side,—of his shroud,— of a stone on which he knelt to pray, and which now bears the impression of his knees,—

of another stone from which he ascended to Heaven, and which bears the print of his feet,—of clothes worn by the Virgin, which represent his portrait,—of the fig-tree on which Judas hanged himself:—in short, of the stone on which St Stephen expired, &c.

In his second book, he passes through various parts of Palestine, visited by pilgrims, and follows them in their errors. When at Jericho, he mentions the house of the harlot Rahab: in the plains of Mamré, he speaks of the tombs of Adam, Abraham, Isaac, Jacob, Sarah, Rebecca and Leah; at Nazareth, he tells us of the spot where the angel came to announce to Mary that, though a virgin, she should conceive; at Bethlehem, of the stone on which JESUS was washed on his nativity,— the tombs of Rachel, David, St Jerome, and of the three shepherds who came to the adoration, &c.

The third book is, for the greater part, dedicated to Constantinople; but he only speaks of the true cross of St George,—of an image of the Virgin which, having been thrown by a Jew into the most disgusting filth, had been picked up by a Christian, and a miraculous oil had flowed from it.

For many ages, the descriptions of Palestine contained nothing but the pious and coarse fables invented daily by the Orientals, to give credit to certain places which they endeavoured to institute as pilgrimages, and thus quietly draw to their own profit the money of the pilgrims. These last greedily swallowed every tale they heard, and scrupulously persevered in paying their devotions at all the places that had been pointed out to them. On their return to Europe, this was all they had to relate: but indeed this was all that was required from them.

Nevertheless our saint (for at his death he was declared such, as well as his editor Adamanus) gives us, in his second book, some historical account of Tyre and Damascus.

He speaks also more in detail respecting Alexandria; and I even find, under the last head, two facts that have seemed to me worthy of attention.

The first concerns the crocodiles, which he represents as so numerous in the lower part of the Nile, that the instant an ox, horse, or ass, enters the river to drink, they are seized by them, and dragged under water and devoured, whilst at this day, if we believe the unanimous accounts of modern travellers, crocodiles are only seen in upper Egypt; and it is a sort of prodigy to see any near to Cairo, and thence to the sea there is not a single one.

The other respects the island of Pharos, on which Ptolomy Philadelphus constructed a tower containing fires, to serve as a land-mark to sailors, and which also had the name of Pharos. It is known that after the time of Ptolomy this island was joined by a mole to the main land, having a bridge at each extremity; that Cleopatra completed the isthmus, by destroying the bridges and carrying on the mole; in short, that at this day the whole island is connected with the main land: nevertheless our prelate speaks of it in his time as if it were still an island, ' In dextera parte portus parva insula habetur, in qua maxima turris est quam, in commune, Græci et Latini, ex ipsius rei usu, Pharum vocitaverunt.' He must doubtless have been mistaken; but probably at the time he saw it the mole only existed, and the immense quantities of earth which make it part of the continent have been since added; and he did not perhaps consider a dyke made by the hand of man capable of preventing an island from being what nature had formed it.

In the ninth century, we had another sort of travels by Hetton, monk and abbot of Richenou, afterward bishop of Basil. He was an able man of business, and employed as such by Charlemagne, who sent him, in 811, ambassador to Constantinople. On his return to France, he there published an account of his mission, which, hitherto, has not been found, and which we ought to regret the more, as it would afford us many curious details respecting an empire, whose connections with France were then so numerous, and carried on with such activity. We should not, perhaps, consider it as totally lost: it may be possible that this manuscript, after remaining many centuries buried, accident may bring to the knowledge of some of our learned men, who will give it to the public.

This has happened to the travels of another french monk, named Bernard, which, being published in 870 and lost, have been found again by Mabillon, and brought to light. Like to those of Arculfus, they consist only of travels to the holy land, more concise, however, than his, and written with less pretension, but with the exception of a few details personal to the author, containing only a dry enumeration of the holy places, which circumstance has caused this likewise to be entitled 'De Locis Sanctis.'

The route, however, of the two pilgrims was different. Arculfus sailed direct for Palestine, and thence re-embarked to visit Alexandria: on the contrary, Bernard first disembarks at Alexandria; he ascends the Nile as far as Babylon, descends it again to Damietta, and, traversing the desert on camels, arrives at Gaza in the holy land.

There he makes, like St Arculfus, different pilgrimages; fewer, however, than the latter, whether from his profession not permitting him such expenses, or whether he has neglected to notice them.

I shall only remark, that in certain churches new miracles had been invented since the time of the bishop,—miracles which he certainly would have mentioned had they then existed; for instance, that of the church of St Mary, wherein it was said no rain ever fell, although it was roofless. Such was the miracle to which the Greeks have given so much celebrity, and which was performed yearly on Easter-eve, in the church of the holy sepulchre, when an angel descended from heaven to light the waxen tapers, furnishing the Christians of the town with a new fire, which was communicated to them by the patriarch, and which they devoutly carried with them to their homes.

Bernard relates an anecdote, in his passage over the desart, deserving notice. He says, that the Christian and pagan merchants had established two caravansaries in this immense ocean of sand,—the one called Albara, the other Albacara,—where travellers might provide themselves with all things necessary for their journey.

This author also informs us of an establishment formed by Charlemagne at Jerusalem, in favour of those who spoke ' la langue romane,' and of the existence of which the French, especially the men of letters, will not hear without a sensible pleasure.

Charlemagne, the glory of the west, had, by his conquests and great qualities, attracted the attention of the celebrated caliph Haroun al-Raschid, a man who had filled the east with his renown.

Haroun, eager to testify to Charles the esteem and consideration he bore him, had sent him ambassadors, with magnificent presents: and these ambassadors, our historians say, were even charged to offer him the keys of Jerusalem, on the part of their master.

Probably Charles had taken advantage of this favourable opportunity to establish an hospital or receptacle in the town for pilgrims who should come from his french territories. Such was the spirit of the times. This sort of travels being thought the most holy that devotion could imagine, a prince who favoured them believed he deserved well from religion. Charlemagne, besides, had a taste for pilgrimages; and his historian, Eginhard, observes with surprise, that in spite of his predilection for St Peter at Rome, he had paid his devotions there but four times in his life.

A great man, however, often shews himself great in the midst of surrounding prejudices. Charles had been the restorer of letters in France: he had re-established orthography, regenerated writing, and formed handsome libraries: he would have his hospital at Jerusalem furnished with a good library also, for the use of the pilgrims; and the establishment was in the entire possession of it at the time of Bernard: ' nobilissimam habens bibliothecam, studio imperatoris.' The emperor had even assigned twelve houses, situated in the valley of Josaphat, with their lands, vineyards and gardens, for the support and repairs of the house, and the maintenance of the pilgrims.

Although Eginhard ought to have been satiated with pilgrimages, he, however, made one to Rome, on his return through Italy, and, when he entered France, another to St Michael's mount.

In regard to this last, he observes that it is situated on a rock on the shore of the coast of Normandy, and washed twice a-day at high water by the waves of the sea. But he adds, that on the feast of the Saint, the access to the rock and to the chapel remains free, and that the ocean forms, like the Red Sea in the time of Moses, two great walls, between which the passage remains perfectly dry; and that this miracle only takes place on this day, and lasts the whole of it.

Our national literature was in possession of four books of travels; one to the coasts of Italy, one to Constantinople, and two to the holy land. In the thirteenth century, a very extraordinary ocurrence procured two to Tartary.

This immense country, whose inhabitants, in various times and under different names, have peopled, conquered, or ravaged the greater part of Europe and Asia, found itself, if I may so say, wholly in arms.

Fanaticised by the incredible conquests of one of their chiefs, the famous Genghis-Khan, and persuaded that the whole earth owed them obedience, these warlike and ferocious wanderers had marched, after the conquest of China, to invade the north-eastern part of Europe.

Wherever their innumerable hordes had passed, kingdoms had been ruined, whole nations exterminated, or dragged into slavery. Hungary, Poland, Bohemia, the frontiers of Austria, were ravaged in a horrible manner. Nothing could check this inundation; and if it felt any resistance in one quarter, it threw itself elsewhere with greater fury. In short, all Christendom was panic-struck; and, to use the expression of one of our historians, ' it trembled to the shores of the ocean *.'

* La Chaise. Vie de St Louis, liv. v. p. 301.

In this general consternation, Innocent IV. wished to shew himself the common father of the faithful. He was, at the time, in Lyons, whither he had come to hold a council for the excommunication of the redoubtable Frederick, who had, three times before, been in vain excommunicated by his predecessors. There, while overwhelming the emperor with all his thunders, Innocent formed a project, the idea alone of which announces his intoxication with power. It was nothing less than to send apostolical letters to the Tartars, to persuade them to lay down their arms, and embrace the Christian religion: ' ut ab hominum strage desisterent, et fidei veritatem reciperent *.' He gives these letters in charge to an ambassador, and this ambassador is a cordelier friar, called Jean du Plan de Carpin, (Joannes de Plano Carpini) who on Easter-day, in the year 1245, sets off with his companions, and,

* Vincent. Bellovac. Spec. Hist. lib. xxxii. cap. 2.

on the road, picks up a third companion, a Polander, named Benedict.

Whether the order of St Dominick was displeased to see such an honour conferred exclusively on the order of St Francis; whether Innocent was alarmed for the safety of his ambassadors in so long and dangerous a journey; or whether, from some other motive of which we are ignorant, he dispatched, by another route, a second embassy, composed solely of preaching friars.——These last, amounting to five, had, for their principal, one named Ascelin; and among them was friar Simon de St Quentin, of whom I shall soon have occasion to speak. They were, like the Cordeliers, bearers of apostolical letters, and were charged with the same orders respecting the Tartars, namely, to prevail on these people to abstain from war of all kinds, and to receive baptism.

De Carpin had, however, with the above instructions, received private and particular ones to examine attentively, and to collect with care, whatever he should think worthy of notice among this people and country. He did so, and, on his return, published a relation composed with this view, and, consequently, entitled by him ' Gesta Tartarorum.' In fact, all he says of his travels, and of what passed on his journey, is comprised in one single chapter. The seven others are filled with descriptions of what relates to the Tartars, as to the soil of their country, their manners, usages, conquests, mode of fighting, &c.

I have discovered, among the manuscripts of the national library, (No 2477, at page 66) a more complete copy than that in Hackluyt, containing a tolerably long preface by the author, not in that edition. In short, at the epocha when these travels first appeared, Vincent de Beauvais had inserted the greater part in his ' Speculum Historiale.'

This friar Vincent, a dominican monk, reader or preacher to St Louis, had been desired by that prince to undertake different works, which in fact he produced, and they now form a very considerable collection. Among the number is a long and heavy historical compilation, under the title of 'Speculum Historiale,' in which he has inserted, or intermixed, the accounts of our traveller. To render it more interesting and complete, he has added, by a very happy thought, certain private details with which he was furnished by his brother-monk, Simon de St Quentin, one of the associates of Ascelin in the second embassy. Having had an opportunity of seeing Simon on his return from Tartary, he learnt from him many things which he has inserted in various parts of his 'Speculum Historiale,' particularly in the thirty-second and last book. There, from what he had written and published of Carpin, and what he had learnt from Simon's conversation, he makes a mixed relation, which he divides into fifty chapters, and this is the account known to us. Bergeron has given a translation of it, in his collection of travels made during the twelfth and three following centuries. He has, however, thought proper to separate the two relations of Carpin and Simon, in order to have memorials of the second embassy as well as of the first. He has, consequently, detached six chapters from the recital of Vincent, attributed by him to Simon, making a separate article of them, under the name of Ascelin, the chief of the second legation, which is all we know of it. As for the success of these two embassies, I do not think it worth mentioning, for it may easily be guessed what it must have been. The same attended two others sent by St Louis to those countries, though from a different motive.

This monarch, in 1248, commenced his disastrous expedition to Egypt, and had just put into the island of Cyprus with his fleet, when he received, on the 12th of December, in that island, an embassy from the Tartars, the two principal persons of which bore the names of David and Mark. These adventurers gave out that they were delegated to him by their prince, who had been lately converted to the Christian faith, and whose name they said was Ercalthay. They likewise affirmed that the great khan of the Tartars had also received baptism, as well as the chief officers of his court and army, and that he was anxious to form an alliance with the king.

However gross this imposture may now seem, Louis could not help swallowing it. He resolved to send an embassy to these converted khans or princes, to congratulate them on their happiness, and to engage them to favour and propagate the Christian religion within their dominions. The ambassador he named for this purpose was a preaching friar, called Andrew Longjumeau, or Lonjumel, to whom he added, as associates, two other Dominicans, two clerks, and two officers of his household.

David and Mark, the better to impose on him, affected to shew themselves fervent Christians: they attended with him all the services for the celebration of Christmas, and gave him to understand that a tent of scarlet cloth would be a most agreeable present to the khan. That was the object of these two knaves. The king instantly ordered a magnificent one to be made, and had embroidered on it the annunciation, the passion, and other mysteries of the Christian religion. To this present he added another, of every thing that was necessary, in vases and in silver plate, for the use of a chapel. In fine, he gave them relics, and some of the wood of the true Cross; that is to say, what was in his opinion above all things in the world.

But here I must not omit an observation, which shews the spirit of that roman court which believed itself to have the right of commanding every sovereign, namely, that the legate whom the pope had placed in the king's army as his representative, and to order all things in his name, wrote, by means of these ambassadors, to the two tartarian princes, and in his letter announced that he adopted and acknowledged them as children of the church. He gained as much from his pretensions, and the advances made in his letter, as the king for his tent, his chapel and his relics. Longjumeau, on his arrival in Tartary, sought in vain for the prince Ercalthay, and this grand khan, who had been baptised with his whole court, and returned as wise as he had set out. He ought, nevertheless, to have gained some knowledge respecting the country; for it was said he had travelled there before, and when David appeared in the presence of the king at Cyprus, he pretended to know him, as having seen him formerly in Tartary. These circumstances have been transmitted to us by the historians of the times. As for himself, he has not left any account of his mission, and it may be thought he was ashamed of it. Louis had been so coarsely duped that he might also have felt some disgust, or at least have gained prudence from experience; but, a very few years after, he again suffered himself to be deceived. It was in the year 1253, when he was still in Asia.

Although, on obtaining his liberty from the prisons of Egypt, he was bound by every tie to return to France, where he had so many wounds to heal and tears to dry, an ill-understood devotion had conducted him to Palestine, where, regardless of the duties he owed his subjects, and to himself as king, he not only lost two years, almost solely occupied in pilgrimages, but, in spite of the exhausted state of the finances of his realm, he expended very considerable sums in rebuilding and fortifying some trifling places of which the Christians of that country were still in the possession.

During this time, a report was current that a tartarian prince, named Sartach, had embraced Christianity. The baptism of an infidel prince was, for Louis, one of those happy circumstances the charms of which it was impossible for him to resist. He therefore determined to send an embassy to Sartach, to compliment him on the occasion, as he had before done to Ercalthay. His former ambassadors were Dominicans; but he now fixed on the Franciscans, and appointed friar Guillaume Rubruquis the principal. Pope Innocent had also successively given an embassy to each of these orders of monks; and to follow such an example was the great delight of Louis. He had so tender an affection for each of them that his sole wish was, he said, to be able to divide himself into two, that he might give to each a half of himself.

Rubruquis, on his arrival at the court of Sartach, might easily have satisfied himself of the falsehood of the tales which the eastern

Christians every now and then propagated, concerning the pretended conversions of tartarian princes. That he might not wholly lose the fruit of his journey, he solicited this chief to permit him to preach the gospel in his dominions. Sartach replied, that he dared not take on himself the granting so extraordinary a request, and sent the converter to his father Baathu, who sent him to the grand khan.

When Rubruquis and his companions presented themselves before this last prince, they were dressed in the copes of the church: one bore a cross and a missal, another a censor, Rubruquis himself the Bible and Psalter, and thus he advanced, supported by them, chaunting canticles. This spectacle which, from his monastic prejudices, he thought imposing, was but a burlesque, and produced no effect, not even the laughter of the Tartar; and, without doubt, ill satisfied with a very useless journey, he returned to give an account of it to the king.

Louis was no longer in Syria. The death of his mother, queen Blanche, had at last recalled him to France, which he ought never to have quitted, but whither, however, he did not return until a further delay of a year. Rubruquis was preparing to follow him, when he received an order from his superior not to leave the country, but to retire to the convent of St Jean d'Acre, and thence to write to the king, to inform him of the ill success of his mission. He obeyed, and sent the king an account, which time has preserved to us, and which, like the preceding one, has been translated by Bergeron. We are indebted for it to the overbearing temper of a jealous and harsh superior; for had the traveller obtained permission to follow the king, and attend his court, he would not, perhaps, have written any thing.

Thus, therefore, of the four monkish embassies sent to Tartary, as well by pope Innocent as the king, the two Franciscans only, Carpin and Rubruquis, have left us any accounts; and these works, although tinged with the modes of thinking of the age, and especially of the profession of those who wrote them, are precious objects to us for the interesting details they give of a distant country, at that time scarcely known by name, and with which, since that epocha, we have not preserved any connection.

The courage of Rubruquis cannot fail of being admired, who fears not to declare openly enough to the king, that David was an impostor who had deceived him. But Louis had the fanaticism of conversions and proselytism; and that, in some minds, is an incurable disorder.

Duped twice, he was so a third time shortly afterward, respecting a king of Tunis, who, he was told, was desirous of receiving baptism. This baptism was a long time his chimera, and he looked forward to the day when he should be god-father to this prince, as the happiest of his life. He would have willingly consented to have passed the remainder of his days in the dungeons of Africa, if, at this price, he could have seen him a Christian. It was for the purpose of standing god-father to an infidel that he sailed to the coasts of Tunis, and lost a second fleet and a second army, and a second time disgraced the french arms, which had shewn such brilliancy at the battle of Bovines, and at last perished by the plague, in the midst of a pestiferous camp, and thus merited, by the multiplied misfortunes of France, the qualifications of martyr and saint.

With regard to Bergeron, every one must agree, that by publishing his translation he has done real service to literature and science; and I am certainly very far from wishing to depreciate the merits of it. I am, however, convinced it would have been greater if he had not made too free a translation of the several pieces that form his collection, and, above all, if he had not omitted so much of the originals, which, indeed, spares us the detail of many uninteresting circumstances, but which, at the same time, deprives us of the inestimable advantage of appreciating the author, and the age he lived in. He himself tells us, in a preliminary discourse to one of the travels which he has printed, 'that he had translated it from very coarse Latin, in which it was written, according to the taste of that age, to display it in our language with more clearness and elegance.' Hence it has happened, that when promising to give us travels of the thirteenth and fourteenth centuries, he has given us modern ones, that have all nearly the same physiognomy, whereas they ought to have had their own proper features.

The collection of Bergeron, though good for his time, is no longer so for ours. As it contains works full of errors, we should wish for notes, historical discussions, and learned remarks; and perhaps a new edition of these ancient travels would be an useful undertaking, and one which could not fail to be well received by the public, more especially if the original text was added to the translation. This translation, however, ought to be scrupulously faithful, and no omissions should be permitted; and extracts ought to be made of such parts as the translator might judge it expedient to retrench. It is not amusement a reader looks for in these works, but instruction. The moment any person attempts to disfigure such authors, by giving to them a modern turn of expression, for the use of the youth of both sexes, their works are ruined. Have you travels, whatever they may be, of such and such a century? This is what I ask, and what you should make me acquainted with.

If there be any one among our men of letters, who, to the knowledge of history and geography, unites courage and patience with the love of research, and whom the above undertaking does not alarm, I inform him, that in regard to the ' Speculum Historiale' there are in the national library four manuscript copies, under the numbers 4898, 4900, 4901, 4902.

The two travellers of the 14th century, who have published their accounts, are not Frenchmen born; but, as both wrote originally in the french language, they belong to us under the title of authors, and, in this respect, I am bound to speak of them. One is Hayton, the Armenian, the other Mandeville, an Englishman.

Hayton, king of Armenia, had been despoiled of his dominions by the Saracens. He applied for succour to the Tartars, who, in fact, took up arms, and re-established him on his throne. His negotiations and his travels appeared to him deserving of being transmitted to posterity, and, in consequence, he drew up some accounts of them, which, when on the point of death, he gave into the hands of Hayton, his nephew, lord of Courchi.

This last, after having taken a very active part, as well in the affairs of Armenia as in the wars which that kingdom had still to support, came to Cyprus, and made himself a Prèmonstré monk. It was in this island he learnt the french language, which, being carried thither by the Lusignans, was become the language of the court, and of all who were not of the lowest orders.

From Cyprus the monk Hayton had passed to Poitiers, where he was desirous of publishing the memoirs of his uncle, and also an account of the events in which he himself had been an actor and witness. He called his work a History of the East, and intrusted the publication of it to another monk, named Faucon, to whom he dictated in French from memory. This work had such success that pope Clement V. ordered the same Faucon to translate it into Latin, that those who did not understand French might not lose the enjoyment of it. The latin translation appeared in 1307; and three manuscript copies of it are in the national library, under the numbers 7514, 7515, A, and 6041. At page 180, at the end of No. 7515, is the following note of the editor, which confirms all that I have said of this book.

' Explicit liber *historiarum partium orientis*, a religioso viro fratre Haytono, ordinis beati Augustini, domino Churchi, consanguineo regis Armeniæ, compilato (compilatus) ex mandato summi pontificis domini Clementis papæ quinti, in civitate Pictaviensi regni Franchie : quem ego Nicolaüs Falconi, primo scripsi in gallico ydiomate, sicut idem frater H. michi (mihi) ore suo dictabat, absque nota sive aliquo exemplari *. Et de Gallico transtuli in Latinum ; anno Domini M.CCC. septimo, mense Augusti.'

Bergeron has published the history of Hayton; but instead of giving the original

* The copy, No. 7514, adds, ' a verbo ad verbum.'

french text, or at least the latin version of the editor, he has merely given a french version of this Latin, so that we have but a translation of a translation.

In regard to Mandeville, he tells us, that this traveller composed his work in three languages, English, French and Latin. It is a mistake, for I have, at this moment, under my eye, a manuscript copy in the national library, No. 10,024, written in 1477, as a note at the conclusion by the copyist assures us. Now in this copy there is the following passage: ' Je eusse mis cest livre en Latin, pour plus briefment delivrez (to proceed more quickly, to abridge the labour). Mais pour ce que plusieurs ayment et entendent mieulx Romans (le François) que Latin, l'ai-ge (je l'ai) mis *en Romans*, affin que chascun l'entende, et que les seigneurs et le chevaliers et aultres nobles hommes qui ne scèvent point de Latin, ou petit, (peu) qui ont esté oultre-mer, saichent se je dy voir (vrai) ou non,'

Besides, at the time of Mandeville, the french language was spoken in England. It had been carried thither by William the conqueror, and none other was allowed to be taught in the schools. All law proceedings, and acts of parliament, were recorded in French; and, when Mandeville wrote in French, it was his natural language. If he had used the Latin, it would have been with a view that other nations, ignorant of French, might read his work.

In truth, his French shews the soil it comes from, by the many anglicisms and vicious expressions, the reasons for which are readily guessed, as it is known that the farther a rivulet flows from its spring-head the more altered the water becomes; but I consider this as the smallest defect of the author: without taste, judgment or criticism, he not only admits into his work, indiscriminately, every tale and fable he hears, but forges the like himself at every moment.

If we believe him, he embarked on Michaelmas-day in the year 1332, and travelled, during thirty-five years, over the greater part of Asia and Africa. Well, reader, have the same courage as I have had, and peruse his book; and if you shall allow that he may perhaps have seen Constantinople, Palestine and Egypt, (which, however, I am far from warranting) you will remain convinced that, most assuredly, he has never set foot in any of those countries which he describes as blindly, viz. Arabia, Tartary, India, Ethiopia, &c.

If the fictions he imagines offered any amusement or interest,—if he only used the right of lying, which the greater part of travellers have so long been in possession of, he might be tolerated; but in his travels the geographical errors are so gross, the fables so stupid, the descriptions of imaginary countries and people so ridiculous,—in short, absurdities so revolting, that I know not what name to give them. It would be disagreeable to treat an author as an impostor; but how much more so to style him an impudent gabbler. Yet how can we otherwise treat a traveller, who tells us of giants *thirty feet high;* of trees whose fruits are changed into birds that are eaten; of other trees that daily spring from the earth, increasing in growth from sun-rise to mid-day, and then decreasing and re-entering the earth in the evenings; of a perilous valley, the fiction of which he had borrowed from our old romances, wherein he meets with such incredible adventures, that he would infallibly have perished, if he had not prudently taken the sacrament; of a river that springs from the terrestrial paradise, and, instead of waters, flows with precious stones. This paradise, which he says is ' au commencement de la terre,' is situated so high, that ' il touche de près la lune.' In short, a thousand other absurdities of the same sort, that mark not the errors of stupidity and credulity, but wilful lies and deceit.

I even consider in the same light the thirty-five years he says he employed to run over the world, without ever thinking of returning to his own country until the gout first tormented him. Although there exist three printed editions of his travels; one of 1487 by Jean Crès, another of 1517 by Regnault, the third of 1542 by Canterel; they are scarcely known but in the short extract Bergeron has published of them. In fact, this editor found them so improbable and so fabulous, that he has reduced them to twelve pages, although our manuscript consists of one hundred and seventy-eight.

In the fifteenth century, we had two other travels to the holy land; the one which I am now about to translate, the other by a carmelite monk named Huen, printed in 1487, but of which I shall not say any thing here, as it is posterior to the other.

The same reason prevents me from noticing a work published by Mamerot, chaunter or canon of Troyes. Beside, this work, entitled ' Passages faiz oultre Mer par les Roys de France et autres Princes et Seigneurs François contre les Turcqs et autres Sarrasins et Mores oultre-marins,' is not, properly speaking, travels, but an historical compilation of the different croisades that took place in France, and which the author, after the false chronicle of Turpin, and our romances of chivalry, has made to commence under the reign of Charlemagne. The national library possesses a magnificent copy of this book, ornamented with a great number of beautiful miniatures and pictures.

I now come to the work of la Brocquière, but this also requires some explanation.

THE

SECOND PART.

———◆———

THE folly of the croisades, like all other follies in France, had but a certain duration; or, to speak more correctly, like to some fevers, it grew calm of itself after a few deliriums. Most assuredly the croisade of Louis le jeune and the two of St Louis, still more disastrous, had brought on the kingdom a sufficiency of shame and misfortunes to have made us believe this fanaticism extinguished for ever. Superstition, nevertheless, sought, from time to time, to rekindle the flame. Often at confession, and in certain cases that required public penance, the clergy imposed, for satisfaction, a pilgrimage to Jerusalem, or a croisade at a certain period.

Many times the popes employed the whole force of their politics, and the ascendancy of their authority, to renew, among the princes of Christendom, one of those *holy leagues*, where their ambition had so much to gain, without risking any thing but indulgencies.

Philippe le bel, through a pretence of zeal and religion, affected, for a moment, to form another croisade in France. Philippe de Valois, a prince the least qualified for so difficult an enterprise, and one which required so much talent, appeared, for some years, to occupy himself on this subject. He received an embassy from the king of Armenia, opened negotiations with the court of Rome, and even ordered preparations for one in the port of Marseille. In short, during the interval of these movements, in the year 1332, a Dominican called Brochard, (sirnamed L'Allemand, from the name of his country) presented him with two latin works composed expressly for this purpose.

In one of them, which consists of a description of the holy land, he makes him acquainted with the country, the object of his intended conquest; and as he had resided twenty-four years in that country, in quality of missionary and preacher, few could allege so many reasons as himself for speaking of it.

The other work, divided into two books, ' Par commémoration des deux épées dont il est mention dans l'Evangile,' subdivided into twelve chapters, ' à l'honneur des douze Apôtres,' treated of the different routes for an army to march thither; of the precautions necessary to be taken for the success of the enterprise; in fine, of the means to be adopted and pursued to insure the undertaking. With regard to this last, which solely concerns the marine, and the art of war, we are surprised to see such subjects handled by an author who was but a simple monk. But who does not know, that in the ages of ignorance, whoever is less ignorant than his contemporaries arrogates to himself the right of discussing every subject? Besides, in the advice Brochard was giving to the king and his generals, his experience may have suggested some useful hints; and, after all, since in the class of nobles, to whom these subjects belonged, no one, perhaps, could be found who had the same local knowlege, and an equal talent for writing on them, why may he not have hazarded that which they were unable to perform?

Whatever we may think of his motive, or the excuse offered, it seems that his work made a favourable impression on the king and his council; for we see, at least by the continuator of the chronicle of Nangis, that the monarch sent, ' in terram Turcorum,' Jean de Cépoy, and the bishop of Beauvais, with a small body of infantry, ' ad explorandos portus et passus, ad faciendas aliquas munitiones et præparationes victualium pro passagio terræ sanctæ;' and that this small troop, after having gained some considerable advantages, considering the weakness of its force, returned to France in the year 1335.

All this noise, however, of armaments, preparations and menaces, with which the kingdom resounded for some years, ended in vain boasting. I doubt not but that, at the beginning, the king was in earnest: he had suffered his vanity to be dazzled by the brilliancy of a project that would fix the eyes of all Asia and Europe on him; and moderate understandings are unable to resist the seduction of such chimeras. But, very soon, like all weak characters, fatigued with difficulties, he sought for a pretext to put an end to it, and, in consequence, demanded from the pope titles and money, which he refused to grant him. The expedition was then no longer talked of; and all it produced was to draw on the king of Armenia the vengeance of the Turks, for having gone to France to solicit a league, and succours against them.

During the following century, similar vain boastings took place at the court of Burgundy, though with a commencement apparently more serious.

In the year 1432, one hundred years after the publication of these two works of Brochard, many great lords in the dominions of Burgundy, and holding offices under duke Philippe le bon, made a pilgrimage to Jerusalem. Among them was his first esquire-carver, named la Brocquière, who, having performed many devout pilgrimages in Palestine, returned sick to Jerusalem, and, during his convalescence, formed the bold scheme of returning to France overland. This would lead him to traverse the western part of Asia and eastern Europe, and, during the whole journey, except towards the end of it, through the dominions of Mussulmen. The execution of such a journey, even at this day, would not be without difficulties, and it was then thought impossible. It was in vain his companions attempted to dissuade him from it: he was obstinate; and, setting out, overcomes every obstacle, returns in the course of the year 1433, and presents himself to the duke in his saracen dress, which he had been obliged to wear, and on the horse that had carried him the whole of this astonishing journey.

So extraordinary an adventure could not fail to produce a great effect at court. The duke had an anxious desire that the traveller should reduce his account to writing, with which he complied; but the work did not appear for some years after, even posterior to the year 1438, since that period is mentioned, as will be seen hereafter.

It was scarcely possible for the duke to have his esquire-carver daily in his presence and not to be sometimes desirous of questioning him about this land of infidels; and as he must have heard his accounts when at table, his imagination could not avoid being heated, and he also must have formed chimeras of croisade and conquest.

What makes me suppose that he put such questions to la Brocquière, is the latter's having inserted in his travels a long discussion on the military force of the Turks,—on the means of combating it successfully,—and concluding, that even a small army, but well organised and conducted, might, without risk, march to Jerusalem. Assuredly such an episode, of so great a length, and with so important a conclusion, deserves notice in a work presented to the duke, and composed by his orders; and we must agree, that it would have scarcely been placed there without design, or without a particular intention.

In fact, we see that from time to time Philippe announced great schemes on this subject; but more occupied with pleasure than with glory, as the fifteen acknowledged bastards he left behind prove, all his vain boastings evaporated in words. At last, however, there was a moment when all Christendom, alarmed at the rapidity of the conquests of the young and formidable Mohammed II. and at the immense armament he was preparing against Constantinople, thought there was no other mode of forming a barrier against him than a general league.

The duke, from the extent and population of his dominions, was more powerful than many kings, and might have acted an important part in this coalition. He affected to make his appearance in it one of the first; and to do it with eclat, he gave, at Lille in 1453, a splendid and pompous feast, or rather spectacle with machinery, altogether very odd, very inconsistent in the multitude of its parts, but the most astonishing of the sort of any that history has handed down to us. This spectacle, which I have elsewhere described *, and which

* M. le Grand d'Aussi refers, in a note, to his ' History of the private Life of the French,' for a description of this festival. As that book may not be much known in this country, I shall translate an account thereof.

swallowed immense sums of money, that, in the present circumstances, might with ease

' Of all the entertainments that history has afforded us any details, there is none which equals that given by Philippe le bon, duke of Burgundy, at Lille, in the year 1453. It displays at once so much magnificence and so many puerilities, such variety of machinery and automata, so many actors and so many living animals, that I believe I shall gratify the curiosity of my readers by describing it. Monstrelet gives an abridged account; but it is detailed at length by Matthieu de Couci and Olivier de la Marche. What, however, renders it interesting, is, that it was occasioned by one great event, and almost the cause of another.

' Mohammed II. one of the most redoubtable and enterprising enemies the Christians had to encounter, menaced, at this moment, Constantinople, which, in fact, he besieged, and took some months afterward. The formidable armament he had prepared for this expedition had made all Europe tremble. It was thought that no other means remained to save Christendom than to form a general league and arm against him; and it was with this intent the duke of Burgundy gave his grand pantomime-entertainment.

' In an immense hall three tables were laid out, that might, perhaps, more justly be called theatres, considering the number of machines that were placed on each. That for the duke was square; and had four ornaments.

' 1. A church with its bell and organ, with four chaunters to play on it, and sing when their time of acting should require it.

' 2. A statue of a naked child, placed on a rock, who from his ' broquette pissait eau-rose.'

have been better employed, concluded with some vows of arms, as well on the part of the

'3. A vessel, larger than what would serve to navigate on the seas, having on board a numerous crew, who performed all the manœuvres as if they had been really at sea.

'4. A rivulet that ran through a meadow ornamented with shrubs and flowers: rocks, studded with saphires and other precious stones, served as a boundary to it; and in the centre was a figure of St Andrew, from the end of whose cross spouted out a stream of water.

'On the second table were seen nine ornaments.

'1. A sort of pasty, in which were inclosed twenty eight musicians, men and children, who were each to play on a different instrument during certain interludes of the feast.

'2. The castle of Lusignan, with its ditches and towers: from the two smallest, a stream of orangeade ran into the ditches; and, on the highest tower, Melusina was seen disguised as a serpent.

'3. A windmill placed on a hillock. A magpie was fixed on one of the sails, which served for a mark to all sorts of persons, who amused themselves with shooting with cross-bows.

'4. A vineyard, in the midst of which were placed two casks, as emblems of those containing good and evil. One held a sweet and the other a bitter liquor. A man richly dressed, seated cross-legged on one of the casks, held in his hand a paper, by which he offered the choice of his liquors to all who might wish to taste them.

'5. A desert country, where a tyger was represented fighting with a serpent.

duke as of several of the lords of his court; and this was the whole result of it. It took

' 6. A savage mounted on a camel, seeming on the point of making a long journey.

' 7. A man with a long pole, beating a bush wherein many small birds had taken refuge. Near to it was an orchard inclosed by a trellis of roses, with a knight seated by his mistress's side, who caught and eat the birds the other drove from the bush. A kind of satirical allegory, ingenious enough, and which probably gave rise to the proverbial expression, ' to beat the bush for another.

' 8. Mountains and rocks covered with hanging icicles, among which a fool was seen mounted on a bear.

' 9. A lake surrounded by various towns and castles. A vessel was on it sailing with all her sails set.

' The third table, smaller than the preceding ones, had but three decorations.

' 1. A travelling merchant, as passing through a village with his pack on his back.

' 2. An indian forest full of automata of various animals walking about.

' 3. A lion fastened to a tree, near which was a man beating a dog.

' On the right and left of the buffet, which was set off with vases of chrystal, cups ornamented with gold and precious stones, and an immense quantity of gold and silver plate, were two columns: one bore the statue of a naked woman, from whose right breast flowed hippocras during supper-time; the lower parts of her body were covered with a napkin loaded with greek letters of a violet colour.

place in February, and Mohammed captured Constantinople in May.

To the other column, a living lion was fastened, by an iron chain. He was there placed to guard the naked woman, as the inscription in golden letters on a shield announced—' Do not touch the lady.'

It is probable the naked woman, with the greek letters, was intended to represent Constantinople despoiled,— the lion, who forbade any one to touch her, the duke of Burgundy,—and the man who beat the dog in presence of the lion, sultan Mohammed.

' Beside the number of machines I have described, the hall contained five scaffolds for those spectators who were not of the supper, and particularly for the great crowds of foreigners whom the report of this feast had brought to Lille.

' On the entrance of the duke and his court, he walked about for some time to examine the various decorations; after which he sat down to table, and the maitres d'hôtel served up the supper.

' Every course consisted of forty-four dishes, each of which was lowered down from the roof by machinery, on cars painted blue and gold, and with the device of the duke.

' The moment he was seated with his guests, the bell of the church tolled, and, instantly, three little choristers came out of the pasty, and began to sing a very sweet air, by way of grace: they were accompanied by a shepherd on his pipe. Shortly after, a horse entered, escorted by fifteen or sixteen knights in the livery of the duke. He moved backward, and bore on his bare back two masked trumpeters, seated back to back; and in this manner he made the circuit of the hall

The news of this disaster, the horrible massacres that followed the conquest, and the

backward, attended by the knights, the two trumpeters playing all the time symphonies.

'When they had quitted the hall, the organ of the church was heard, and one of the musicians in the pasty played on a german horn. A great automata, representing an enormous wild boar, now entered, having on his back a monster, half a savage and half a griffin; and this monster bore also a man on his shoulders. They had no sooner departed than the chaunters in the church sang an air, and three of the musicians in the pasty executed a trio: one played on the douçaine (dulciana, probably dulcimer), the second on the lute, and the third on another instrument.

'Such were the different amusements that formed the accompaniments to the first course: all, excepting the music, were farces foreign to the feast. Those of the second course had as little connection; but they were preparatory to the last, in which the object of this entertainment was to be pathetically explained.

'The entertainment of the second course consisted of a dramatic pantomime that represented the conquest of the golden fleece by Jason,—a kind of allegory that recalled to the spectators the order of the golden fleece, which the duke had instituted twenty-three years before.

For this spectacle, a small theatre had been erected at one end of the hall, and which a large green silken curtain had hid from the eyes of the assembly. On a sudden, a symphony of clarions was heard behind this curtain: it was drawn up, and Jason was seen fighting with, and bringing to the yoke.

incalculable consequences it might have on Christendom, spread universal alarm. The

two bulls that vomited flames of fire, to whom had been committed the defence of the garden of the Hesperides. The hero next combats a monstrous dragon, cuts off his head and tears out his teeth. He then ploughs a field with the bulls he had tamed, sows there the teeth of the dragon, and instantly an army of soldiers spring from the earth, who fight together most bitterly, and alternately kill each other.

'The three acts of this sort of opera did not immediately follow: the spaces between each act were filled up by interludes in the taste of those of the preceding. The first consisted of a youth who entered the hall mounted on a large white stag, when they both sang a duo; then a fiery dragon, who flew round the hall. A hawking scene was next presented, when two falcons were seen to strike down a heron, which was instantly presented to the duke. All these interludes were accompanied either by pieces on the organ, by the chaunters in the church, or by the musicians in the pasty, who every time executed an air on a different instrument.

'These successive spectacles, however, were but, as I have said, a preliminary amusement,—or, to borrow the expressions of the two authors from whom I make this extract, were but ' a worldly pastime,' given to the spectators to entertain them until the time of the grand scene, the scene which was to explain the subject of this feast, and the real cause of it.

'It was opened by a giant dressed with a turban in the morisco fashion, and clothed in a long robe of striped green duke then thought it incumbent on him to declare his intentions otherwise than by feasts,

silk. He held in his left hand a guisarme of the antique mode, and with his right led an elephant. This animal bore on its back a tower in which was a female to represent the church: she had on her head a white veil, after the manner of nuns: her robe was of white satin, but her mantle was black, to mark her grief. When she was come near to where the duke sate, she sang a triolet to have the giant stopped, and then made a long complaint in verse, in which having displayed the many ills she was suffering from the infidels, she implored succour from the duke and the knights of the fleece then present.

' Different officers now entered with the king at arms, of the order of the golden fleece, followed by two knights of the order, each leading a damsel, one of whom was natural daughter to the duke. The king at arms bore a live pheasant, decorated with a collar of gold and precious stones: approaching the duke, he made a profound obeisance, and said, that it being the custom at grand festivals to offer to the princes and gentlemen a peacock, or some noble bird, for them to make a vow upon, he was come with two ladies to offer to his valour a pheasant.

' The duke, in reply to this proposition, gave to the king at arms a billet written in his own hand, that he had prepared beforehand, the substance of which was read aloud, as follows. He there vowed, to God pre-eminent, then to the glorious virgin, his mother, and afterward to the ladies, and to the pheasant, that if the king of France, his lord paramount, or any other princes, would undertake a croisade against the Turks, he would accompany or follow them; and that he himself and announced a croisade. He consequently levied large sums from his people, even formed an army, and marched into Germany: but on

would combat the sultan body to body, if he would accept his challenge. The lady representing the church having thanked him, she made the circuit of the hall with her elephant, during which time almost all the princes and great lords present made vows on the bird of the most extravagant nature—such as not to drink wine, not to be seated at table, or not to lie down one day of the week, until they should have met the infidel army—or have been the first to attack it—or have overthrown the banner of the sultan—or to return to Europe without bringing with them a Turk prisoner. In short, one made a vow, (which will give an idea of the religion of these new croisaders) that if he could not obtain the last favours of his mistress before his departure, he would marry the first damsel he should meet that had twenty thousand crowns.

'When the vows were ended, a troop of musicians entered, accompanied by a great number of lighted torches. Twelve ladies followed, every one attended by a knight: each personified a virtue. They formed a dance, and thus the festival ended.

'All this noisy vain boasting had no effect. The duke levied large sums from his territories under pretence of this croisade, and even advanced into Germany, when a convenient illness made him return home; and this pretended lion permitted Mohammed to beat the dog without any opposition.'

For further particulars, see 'l'Histoire de la Vie privée des François.'

a sudden the raging lion stopped,—a very convenient illness served for a pretext, and he returned home again.

He nevertheless affected to talk of croisades as before, and ordered one of his subjects, Joseph Miélot, canon of Lille, to translate for him into French the two treatises of Brochard that I have before noticed. In short, when pope Pius II. convoked at Mantua, in 1459, an assembly of Christian princes, to form a league against Mohammed, he did not fail to send thither his ambassadors, at the head of whom was the duke of Cleves.

Miélot finished his work in 1455, as the short preface at the beginning informs us: the two translations are in one of the manuscripts which the national library has lately received from Belgium. They are written in the same hand with the travels of la Brocquière.

Although of the three works, this ought to have appeared before the other two, nevertheless the whole three, whether from economy in binding or from analogy of matters, have been united together, and thus form a thick folio volume, numbered 314, bound in wood, covered with red sheepskin, and lettered on the back, ' Avis directif de Brochard.'

This manuscript, from the writing, preservation, miniatures, and fineness of the vellum, is very valuable; but its value is greatly increased by other considerations, for in my opinion it has been composed from original treatises presented by their authors to Philippe le bon, or from the copy commanded by him to be made by one of his copyists from the handwriting of the authors, placed perhaps in his library.

I think I see a confirmation of this assertion, not only in the beauty of the MS. and in the escutcheon of the prince, which is emblazoned in four places, and twice with his motto, ' Aultre n'aray,' but also in the vignette of one of the two frontispieces, as well as in the miniature of the other. This vignette, which is at the beginning of the volume, represents Miélot on his knees presenting his book to the duke, who is seated and surrounded by several courtiers, three of whom are decorated, like himself with the collar of the golden fleece. In the miniature preceding the travels, la Brocquière is seen in the same attitude. He is dressed as a Saracen, and has near him his horse, which I have before mentioned.

With regard to duke Philip, sirnamed the Good, this is not the place to examine whether he has truly deserved so glorious a title, and whether history has not many reproaches to make him of more than one kind. But, as a man of letters, I must not omit saying, in honour to his memory, that learning has many obligations to him, and that he was one of the princes from Charlemagne to Francis I. who have done the most for it; that in the fifteenth century he was in the two Burgundies, and in Belgium particularly, what in the preceding century Charles V. had been in France, and that, like Charles, he had formed for himself a library; had ordered translations and original works; had encouraged men of letters, draughtsmen and able copyists; in fine, that he perhaps rendered to the sciences more real services than Charles, because he was less superstitious.

I shall give, in ' the History of French Literature,' which I am now writing, details on all these different facts. I have discovered numerous proofs of them in the manuscripts that have passed from Belgium to France, or, to speak more correctly, in the manuscripts of the library from Brussels, which constituted one of the most considerable parts of what came from that country. This library, which in regard to the french part of it, is especially confided to my care, and consequently has been almost wholly perused by me, was composed from the libraries of private persons, of whom the principals are as follow:

1*mo*, A certain number of manuscripts that had formerly composed the library of Charles V. of Charles VI. of John duke of Berri, brother to Charles V. and which, during the troubles of the kingdom under Charles VI. and at the beginning of the reign of his son, were stolen and carried away by the dukes of Burgundy. Those of John are known from his signature, written by himself on the last page of the volume, and sometimes in many other places. Those that belonged to the two kings of France have the shield of France emblazoned, and have dedicatory epistles, with miniatures, representing the authors presenting their books to the monarch, who is clothed in the royal mantle. There are other manuscripts, taken from the foregoing libraries, but for the theft of them I cannot produce such authentic proofs, because, in the number, many are not ornamented with miniatures, or had not been presented to the king, and therefore bear not such marks as those before mentioned; but I can produce, in proof that they have been acquired by the like means, so many probabilities, and plausible conjectures, that they are, in my eyes, equivalent to proof-positive.

2do, Manuscripts that legitimately belonged to the dukes of Burgundy, that is to say, which were either acquired by them, or dedicated and presented to them, or commanded by them, whether as original works or as simple copies. In the class of those dedicated, the greater number have been inscribed to Philippe le bon. Of those written by command, almost the whole were for him; and this confirms what I before said, of the obligations literature has to him, and what he did for it.

3tio, Manuscripts, which having belonged to great lords in the dominions of Burgundy, or to private persons, have passed at different times, and by some means or other, into the Brussels library. Among them, we must particularly notice those of Charles de Croy, count of Chimay, godfather to the emperor

Charles V. knight of the golden fleece, created by Maximilian, in 1486, prince of Chimay. His manuscripts are pretty numerous, and bear, for a distinctive mark, his arms, and his signature written by himself.

It results from the above, that in regard to the merits of the Brussels collection in French, it can scarcely offer any but modern manuscripts. I have indeed seen very few that were valuable for their antiquity, their rarity, or the subject of the work; but many are curious for their writing, their preservation, and especially for their miniatures; and these last will be interesting objects to persons who, like me, shall undertake a history of the arts in the lower ages. They will prove, that in Belgium the flourishing state of some manufactures had considerably advanced the progress of the arts of painting and drawing. But I return to the three treatises of our volume.

I shall say but one word on Brochard's description of Palestine, because the original

Latin having been printed it is known, and because Miélot, in the preface to his translation, assures us, of what I am myself convinced of, that he has not added any thing of his own. Brochard, on his part, insists on his exactness. He not only remained twenty-four years in that country, but traversed it in its double diameter from north to south, from the foot of Libanus to Beersheba,—and from west to east, from the Mediterranean to the Dead Sea. In short, he describes nothing, which to use the words of his translator, ' he had not bodily seen, he himself being on the spot.'

The translation begins at page 76 of our volume, and has this title: ' Le livre de la description de la terre-saincte, fait en l'onneur et loenge de Dieu, et compilé jadis, l'an M. IIIc XXXII. par frere Brochard, l'Alemant, de l'ordre des Prescheurs.'

His second work being unpublished, I shall speak of it more fully, but solely from the translation by Miélot. The work is divided into two parts, and is entitled, 'Advis directif,' (counsels for marching) pour faire le passage d'oultre mer.'

For this expedition, says Brochard, there are two different ways, by land and by sea; and he advises the king to use them both at the same time,—the first for his army, the second for the transport of provision, tents, machines and ammunitions of war, and for such as are accustomed to the sea. This would require from ten to twelve galleys, which by negotiations may be obtained from the Genoese or Venetians. These last have possession of Candia, Negropont with other islands and important places on the continent. The Genoese have Pera, near to Constantinople, and Caffa in Tartary. These two nations are beside well acquainted with the winds and seas of Asia, with the language, the islands, shores and ports of that country.

Should the voyage by sea be preferred, the ports of Aigues-mortes, Marseille or Nice may be chosen to embark from; and the island of Cyprus would serve for a harbour to receive them, in like manner as St Louis put in there. But many inconveniencies arise from a sea voyage, as well as the remaining so long on board ship, which generally causes disagreeable sicknesses in man and horse. This voyage must depend also on the winds, and there is always reason to fear tempests, and the ill effects of change of climate. It even often happens, that when it is intended merely to put into a port, the vessel is detained by contrary winds. Add to these dangers, the wines of Cyprus, which are naturally too ardent: if you mix water with them, you destroy their flavour,—and if you do not, they affect the brain and burn the entrails. When St Louis wintered in this island, his army suffered all these inconveniences; for there died two hundred and fifty counts, barons and knights, of the highest nobility in his army.

There is another passage, including sea and land, and which offers two roads,—the one through Africa, the other through Italy. That through Africa is extremely dangerous, on account of the fortified castles near which you must march, the risk of wanting provision, the desert you must pass through, and Egypt. The road itself is also of an immense length; for if you set out from the streights of Gibraltar, you will have 2500 miles to march before you can arrive within two short days journey of Jerusalem: if you set out from Tunis, 2400. Conclusion—the road through Africa is impossible, and must not be thought of.

The route through Italy presents three different roads: one through Aquileia, Istria, Dalmatia, the kingdom of Rassia (Servia), and Thessalonica, *the greatest city of Macedonia,* which is but eight short days journey from Constantinople. This was the route followed by the Romans, when they made war in the east. These countries are fertile, ' but inhabited by people disobedient to the church of Rome. With regard to their valour and boldness to resist, they are beneath notice, not being in any respect superior to women.'

The second is through la Puglia. The embarkation must take place at Brundusium, to disembark at Durazzo, which belongs to my lord the prince of Tarentum. The army would then advance through Albania, Blaque and Thessalonica.

The third, in like manner, traverses la Puglia; but it passes through Otranto, Corfou, which belongs to my foresaid lord of Tarentum, Desponte, Blaque, Thessalonica. This was the road followed at the first croisade by Robert earl of Flanders, Robert duke of Normandy, Hugh brother to king Philippe I. and Tancred prince of Tarentum.

After discussing the passages by sea, and by sea and land, Brochard examines the one wholly by land. It traverses Germany, Hungary and Bulgaria, and was taken by the greater part of the armies of France and Germany at the first croisade, under the conduct of Peter the hermit, and is that which the author advises the king to follow. But when in Hungary there is the choice of two roads; the one through Bulgaria—the other through Sclavonia, which constitutes part of the kingdom of Rassia. Godfrey of Bouillon, his two brothers, and Baldwin count of Mons, took the first road. Raimond comte de Saint Gilles, and Audemare bishop of Puy, and legate from the holy see, followed the second, although some authors pretend that they took that through Acquileia and Dalmatia.

Should the king adopt this passage overland, the army, when in Hungary, might be divided into two, and then, for the greater convenience of forage, each party might take separate roads; the one through Bulgaria, the other through Sclavonia. The king should follow the first road, as being the shortest. With regard to the Languedocians and Provençals, who are near to Italy, they may be permitted to go by way of Brundusium and Otranto. Their rendezvous would be at Thessalonica, where they would meet the main body which had marched through Aquileia. To this advice, as to the advantages and inconveniences of the different roads, the Dominican adds some others respecting the princes through whose states it would be necessary to pass, and on the resources which may be found in these several states.

La Rassia, he says, is a fertile country, with five gold mines, five of silver, and many more producing gold and silver, at work No more than one thousand horse and six thousand infantry, would be wanted for the conquest of this country, and ' it would be an agreeable and acceptable jewel to gain.'

The author wishes that no treaty of alliance should be made with this king, nor with the greek emperor; and, the better to strengthen his proposition, he relates some particulars as to the persons of these two monarchs, and especially of the first, whom he calls an usurper. As for the other, he not only insists that neither peace nor truce should be made, but that war should be declared against him.

In consequence, he points out the means to besiege Constantinople, Adrianople and Thessalonica; and as from what has happened, he no way doubts of what may again happen, that is to say, the capture of Constantinople, he proposes divers regulations for the government of the empire of the east, when it shall be a second time conquered, and for bringing it again under the roman religion.

He concludes his ' Avis directifs,' by warning the croisaders to be on their guard against the perfidy of the Greeks, as well as against the Syrians, the Hassassins, and other people of Asia. He enters into a detail of the plots that will be laid for them, and shews the manner of avoiding them.

Brochard, in his first part, has conducted *the host of our Lord* by land to Constantinople, and made it capture the town. In the second part, he causes it to pass the Dardanelles, and leads it into Asia. He is, however, perfectly acquainted with these countries; for, independently of his twenty-four years residence in Palestine, he had travelled over Armenia, Persia, the grecian empire, &c.

According to him, the cause of the ill success of the kings of France and England, in the preceding croisades, was the ill-judged attacks they made on the Turks and the sultan of Egypt at the same time. He proposes to make war only on the Turks, and to have them alone for enemies. To do it with success, he gives descriptions of Turkey, called by the Greeks, Anachèly (Anatolia). He points out the means of securing provision for the army by sea, and gives the well-founded hope of victory over a people necessarily abandoned by God, because *their malice is accomplished*, and internally weakened by intestine wars, and from the want of leaders,—whose cavalry is composed of slaves, having little courage or industry, with small weak horses, badly armed with turkish bows and haubergeons of leather, which may more properly be called cuirasses *; over a people, in short, who only fight as they retreat, and who, after the Greeks and Babylonians, are the most worthless of all the east in deeds of arms.

The author declares, at the conclusion, that in all that country there is scarcely a nation which he has not seen march to battle; and that the single power of France, without any aid whatever, may defeat, not only the Turks and Egyptians †, but also the Tartars, excepting solely the Indians, Arabians and Persians.

The Brussels collection contains another copy of the ' Advis directif,' on paper in folio,

* The haubert and haubergeon (a lighter sort of haubert) were a kind of netted shirts of iron, which fell half way down the thigh. The turkish haubergeons, on the contrary, were so short, they might, according to our author, be called by the name of cuirasses.

† The Turks and Egyptians!! friar Brochard, you forget Louis le jeune and St Louis.

with miniatures, No 352. This makes a volume of itself. The vignette represents Brochard writing at his desk; and in the next miniature, he is presenting his book to the king: this is followed by another miniature, where the king is seen on his march to the holy land.

I have also found, in the same collection, the two latin treatises of the author, united in one volume folio on paper, No. 319, bound in red sheepskin. The title of the first is ' Directorium ad passagium faciendum, editum per quemdam fratrem ordinis predicatorum, scribentem experta et visa potius quam audita; ad serenissimum principem et dominum Philippum regem Francorum, anno Domini M.CCC.XXXII.'

The title of the second is, ' Libellus de terra sancta, editus a fratre Brochardo, Theutonico, ordinis fratrum predicatorum.' At the end of this copy, we read that it was written by Jean Reginaldi, canon of Cambray,

As the other is undoubtedly of the same handwriting, I am convinced it must also have been written by Reginaldi.

It now remains for me to make my readers acquainted with our third french work, the travels of la Brocquière, which I am about to publish.

The author was a gentleman, as may easily be seen, when he speaks of horses, strong castles, and tiltings. His account is but an itinerary, which is often somewhat monotonous, particularly in the descriptions of countries and towns; but this itinerary is interesting to the history and the geography of the times. There will be found in them very precious materials, and sometimes sketches and pictures not without merit.

The traveller is a man of a prudent and sensible mind, full of judgment and understanding. The impartiality he displays, when he speaks of the infidel nations with which he has had occasion to be acquainted, will be admired, particularly his account of the Turks, whose good faith, according to him, was greatly superior to that of many Christians. He has scarcely any of the superstition of his age, but the devotion to pilgrimages and relics: at the same time, he shews little faith in the authenticity of the relics which were displayed before him.

With regard to pilgrimages, it will be seen by the perusal of his book how they had been multiplied in Palestine; and his work will be for us a memorial which, on one hand, will convince us of the blind credulity of our western devotees in adopting these pious fables, and, on the other hand, of the criminal tricks of the Christians in the holy land, who had invented them to wheedle out the money from the pockets of the croisaders and pilgrims, and gain an income at their expense.

La Brocquière writes, like a military man, in a frank and manly style, which announces veracity and inspires confidence; but he also writes negligently, so that his subject is not always very clearly arranged, and at times he begins to relate a fact, the continuation of which is in some distant pages. Though this confusion be rare, I have taken the liberty to correct, and to unite what was before divided.

Our manuscript has the same defect as the greater part of other manuscripts, in the orthography of certain names, which frequently vary in every page, and even sometimes in two sentences that follow each other. I may be blamed, perhaps, for noticing these variations of a language which, though at that time instable, is now fixed; for instance, he writes, *Auteriche*, *Autherich*, *Austrice*, and *Ostriche*.

This I have corrected, and shall do the same with those names the spelling of which does not vary in the manuscript, but which are differently written at this day. Other names are completely changed, and are no longer the same. We do not now call the Black Sea 'la Mer Majeure,' nor the Danube 'la Dunoë.'

I am aware that it will be matter of objection against me, that I have done wrong in giving to an author expressions which were neither his own, nor those of his time; but having well weighed the advantages and inconveniences of a very literal translation, I have been satisfied that so rigorous an exactness would render the text unintelligible and fatiguing for the generality of readers; and that, if we would have an author understood, we must make him speak as he would have spoken himself, had he been living among us. In short, there are things of which good sense ordains the suppression or change; and it would be ridiculous, for instance, to say like la Brocquière, ' un seigneur hongre,' for ' un seigneur hongrois;' ' des Chretiens vulgaires,' for ' des Chretiens bulgares,' &c.

THE TRAVELS OF LA BROCQUIERE.

HERE BEGINS THE JOURNEY OF BERTRANDON DE LA BROCQUIÈRE TO THE HOLY LAND, IN THE YEAR OF GRACE ONE THOUSAND FOUR HUNDRED AND THIRTY-TWO.

To animate and inflame the hearts of such noble men as may be desirous of seeing the world, and by the order and command of the most high, most powerful, and my most redoubted lord, Philippe, by the grace of God, duke of Burgundy, Lorraine, Brabant and Limbourg, count of Flanders, Artois and

Burgundy*, palatine of Hainault, Holland, Zealand and Namur, marquis of the holy empire, lord of Friesland, Salins and Mechlin, I, Bertrandon de la Brocquière, a native of the duchy of Guienne, lord de Vieux-Chateau, counsellor, and first esquire-carver to my aforesaid most redoubted lord, after recollecting every event, in addition to what I had made an abridgement of in a small book by way of memorandums, have fairly written out this account of my short travels, in order that if any king, or Christian prince, should wish to make the conquest of Jerusalem, and lead thither an army overland, or if any gentleman should be desirous of travelling thither, each of them may be made acquainted with all the towns, cities, regions, countries, rivers, mountains and passes in the districts, as

* Burgundy was divided into two parts, the duchy and county. The last, since known under the name of Franche Comté, began, at this period, to take that appellation; and this is the reason why our author styles Philippe duke and count of Burgundy.

well as the lords to whom they belong, from the duchy of Burgundy to Jerusalem.

The route hence to the holy city of Rome is too well known for me to stop and describe it. I shall pass lightly over this article, and not say much until I come to Syria. I have travelled through the whole country from Gaza, which is the entrance to Egypt, to within a day's journey of Aleppo, a town situated on the north of the frontier, and which we pass in going to Persia.

Having formed a resolution to make a devout pilgrimage to Jerusalem, and being determined to discharge my vow, I quitted, in the month of February, in the year 1432, the court of my most redoubted lord, which was then at Ghent. After traversing Picardy, Champagne, Burgundy, I entered Savoy, crossed the Rhône, and arrived at Chambery by the Mont-du-Chat.

Here commences a long chain of mountains, the highest of which is called

Mount Cenis, which forms a dangerous pass for travellers in times of snow. The road is so difficult to find, that a traveller, unless he wish to lose it, must take one of the guides of the country, called ' Marrons.' These people advise you not to make any sort of noise that may shake the atmosphere round the mountain, for in that case the snow is detached, and rolls with impetuosity to the ground. Mount Cenis separates Italy from France.

Having thence descended into Piedmont, a handsome and pleasant country, surrounded on three sides by mountains, I passed through Turin, where I crossed the Po, and proceeded to Asti, which belongs to the duke of Orleans; then to Alexandria, the greater part of the inhabitants of which are said to be usurers,—to Piacenza, belonging to the duke of Milan,—and at last to Bologna la Grassa, part of the pope's dominions. The emperor Sigismund was at Piacenza: he had come thither from Milan, where he had received his second crown, and was on his road to Rome in search of the third

From Bologna I had another chain of mountains (the Appenines) to pass, to enter the states of the Florentines. Florence is a large town, where the commonalty govern. Every three months they elect for the government magistrates, called Priori, who are taken from different professions; and as long as they remain in office they are honoured, but on the expiration of the three months they return to their former situations.

From Florence I went to Monte Pulciano, a castle built on an eminence, and surrounded on three sides by a large lake (Lago di Perugia),

---

* In 1414 Sigismund, elected emperor, had received the silver crown at Aix la Chapelle. In the month of November 1431, a little before the passage of our traveller, he had received the iron crown at Milan; but it was not until 1443 he received at Rome, from the hands of the pope, that of gold.

thence to Spoleto, Monte-Fiascone, and at length to Rome.

Rome is well known. Authors of veracity assure us, that for seven hundred years she was mistress of the world. But although their writings should not affirm this, would there not be sufficiency of proof in all the grand edifices now existing; in those columns of marble, those statues, and those monuments as marvellous to see as to describe.

Add to the above the immense quantities of relics that are there,—so many things that our Lord has touched, such numbers of holy bodies of apostles, martyrs, confessors and virgins,—in short, so many churches where the holy pontiffs have granted full indulgences for sin.

I saw there Eugenius IV. a Venetian, who had just been elected pope *. The prince of

* We shall see, hereafter, that la Brocquière left Rome on the 25th march, and Eugenius had been elected on the first days of the month.

Salernum had declared war against him: he was of the Colonna family, and nephew to pope Martin *.

I quitted Rome the 25th of March, and, passing through a town belonging to the count de Thalamoné, a relation to the cardinal des Ursins, arrived at Urbino; thence, through the lordships of the Malatestas, came to Rimini, part of the venetian dominions. I crossed three branches of the Po, and came to Chiosa, a town of the Venetians, which had formerly a good harbour; but this was destroyed by themselves, when the Genoese came to lay siege to Venice. From Chiosa, I landed at Venice, distant twenty-five miles.

Venice is a great and handsome town, ancient and commercial, and built in the

---

* Martin V. predecessor to Eugenius, was a Colonna; and there was a declared enmity between his family and that of the Orsini. Eugenius, when established in the holy chair, took part in this quarrel, and sided with the Orsini against the Colonnas, who were nephews to Martin. The last took up arms, and made war on him.

middle of the sea. Its different quarters being separated by water form so many islands, so that a boat is necessary to go from one to the other.

This town possesses the body of St Helena, mother of the emperor Constantine, as well as many others that I have seen, especially several bodies of the holy innocents, which are entire. These last are in an island called Murano, renowned for its manufactories of glass.

The government of Venice is full of wisdom. No one can be a member of the council, nor hold any employment, unless he be noble and born in the town. It has a duke, who is bound to have ever with him, during the day, six of the most ancient and celebrated members of the council. When the duke dies, his successor is chosen from among those who have shewn the greatest knowledge and zeal for the public good.

On the 8th of May, I embarked to accomplish my vow, on board a galley, with some other pilgrims. We coasted Sclavonia, and successively touched at Pola, Zara, Sebenico and Corfou.

Pola seemed to me to have been formerly a handsome and strong town, with an excellent harbour. We were shewn at Zara the body of St Simeon, to whom our Lord was presented in the Temple. The town is surrounded on three sides by the sea, and its fine port is shut in by an iron chain. Sebenico belongs to the Venetians, as does Corfou, which, with a very handsome harbour, has also two castles.

From Corfou we sailed to Modon, a good and fair town in the Morea, under the same masters; thence to Candia, a most fertile island, the inhabitants of which are excellent sailors. The government of Venice nominates a governor, who takes the title of duke, but who holds his place only three years. Thence to Rhodes, where I had but time to see the town: to Baffa, a ruined town in the island of Cyprus,—and at length to Jaffa, in the holy land of promise.

At Jaffa, the pardons commence for pilgrims to the holy land. It formerly belonged to the Christians, and was then strong: at present, it is entirely destroyed, having only a few tents covered with reeds, whither pilgrims retire to shelter themselves from the heat of the sun. The sea enters the town, and forms a bad and shallow harbour: it is dangerous to remain there long for fear of being driven on shore by a gust of wind. There are two springs of fresh water; but one is overflowed by the sea, when the westerly wind blows a little strong. When any pilgrims disembark there, interpreters and other officers of the sultan * instantly hasten to ascertain their numbers, to serve them as guides, and

* The sultans of Egypt are here meant. Palestine and Syria were at that time under their power. The sultan will be often mentioned in the course of the work.

to receive, in the name of their master, the customary tribute.

Ramlé, the first town we came to from Jaffa, is without walls, but a good and commercial town, seated in an agreeable and fertile district. We went to visit, in the neighbourhood, a village where my lord Saint George was martyred; and, on our return to Ramlé, we continued our route, and arrived, after two days, at 'the holy city of Jerusalem, where our Lord JESUS CHRIST suffered death for us.'

After performing the customary pilgrimages, we performed those to the mountain where JESUS fasted forty days; to the Jordan, where he was baptised; to the church of Saint John, near to that river; to that of Saint Martha and St Mary Magdalen, where our Lord raised Lazarus from the dead; to Bethlehem, where he was born; to the birth place of St John Baptist; to the house of Zachariah; and, lastly, to the holy cross, where the tree grew that formed the real cross, after which we returned to Jerusalem.

The Cordeliers have a church at Bethlehem, in which they perform divine service, but they are under great subjection to the Saracens. The town is only inhabited by Saracens, and some Christians of the girdle *.

At the birth-place of St John Baptist, a rock is shewn, which, during the time of Herod's persecution of the innocents, opened itself miraculously in two, when St Elizabeth having therein hid her son, it closed again of itself, and the child remained shut up, as it is said, two whole days.

Jerusalem is situated in a mountainous and strong country, and is at this day a considerable

---

* The caliph Motouakkek, in the year 235 of the Hegira, or the 856th of the Christian æra, ordered the Christians and Jews to wear a broad girdle of leather, and they wear it to this day in the east. From that epocha, the Christians of Asia, and especially those of Syria, who are mostly Jacobites, or Nestorians, were called Christians of the Girdle.

town, although it appears to have been much more so in former times. It is under the dominion of the sultan, to the shame and grief of Christendom. Among the free Christians, there are but two Cordeliers who inhabit the holy sepulchre, and even they are harrassed by the Saracens: I can speak of it from my own knowledge, having been witness of it for two months. In the church of the holy sepulchre reside also many other sorts of Christians: Jacobites, Armenians, Abyssinians from the country of Prester John, and Christians of the girdle; but of these the Francs suffer the greatest hardships.

When all these pilgrimages were accomplished, we undertook another, equally customary, that to St Catherine's on Mount Sinai. For this purpose we formed a party of ten pilgrims, sir André de Thoulongeon, sir Michel de Ligne, Guillaume de Ligne, his brother, Sanson de Lalaing, Pierre de Vaudrey, Godefroi de Thoisi, Humbert Buffart, Jean de la Roe, Simonet (his family name is left blank) and myself*.

For the information of others, who like myself, may wish to visit this country, I shall say, that the custom is to treat with the chief interpreter at Jerusalem, who receives a tax for the sultan, and one for himself, and then sends to inform the interpreter at Gaza, who, in his turn, negotiates a passage with the Arabians of the desert. These Arabs enjoy the right of conducting pilgrims; and, as they are not always under due subjection to the sultan, their camels must be used, which they let to hire at ten ducats a head.

The Saracen, who at this time held the office of chief interpreter, was called

---

* These names, of which the five first are of great lords in the states of the duke of Burgundy, shew that several persons of the duke's court had formed a company for this pilgrimage to Palestine, and are, probably, those who embarked with our author at Venice, although he has not before named them. Toulongeon was created, this same year 1432, a knight of the golden fleece, but was not invested with the order; for he was then a pilgrim, and died on the road.

Nanchardin. Having received the answer from the Arabs, he assembled us before the chapel, which is at the entrance and on the left of the holy sepulchre: he there took down in writing our ages, names, surnames, and very particular descriptions of our persons, and sent a duplicate of this to the chief interpreter at Cairo. These precautions are taken for the security of travellers, and to prevent the Arabs from detaining any of them; but I am persuaded that it is done likewise through mistrust, and through fear of some exchange or substitution that may make them lose the tribute-money.

When on the eve of our departure, we bought wine for the journey, and laid in a stock of provision, excepting biscuit, which we were to find at Gaza. Nanchardin having provided asses and mules to carry us and our provision, with a particular interpreter, we set off.

The first place we came to was a village formerly more considerable, at present inhabited by Christians of the girdle, who cultivate vines. The second was a town called St Abraham, and situated in the valley of Hebron, ' where our Lord created our first father Adam.' In that place are buried together, Abraham, Isaac and Jacob, with their wives; but this sepulchre is now inclosed within a mosque of the Saracens. We were anxious to see it, and even advanced to the gate; but our guides and interpreter assured us they dared not suffer us to enter in the day-time, on account of the dangers they should run, and that any Christian found within a mosque is instantly put to death, unless he renounce his religion.

After the valley of Hebron, we traversed another of greater extent, near to which the mountain whereon St John performed his penitence was pointed out to us. Thence we crossed a desert country, and lodged in one of those houses built through charity, and called Khan: from this khan, we came to Gaza.

Gaza, situated in a fine country near the sea, and at the entrance of the desert, is a strong town, although uninclosed. It is pretended that it formerly belonged to the famous Samson. His palace is still shewn, and also the columns of that which he pulled down; but I dare not affirm that these are the same.

Pilgrims are harshly treated there; and we should have likewise suffered, had it not been for the governor, a man about sixty years of age, and a Circassian, who heard our complaints, and did us justice. Thrice were we obliged to appear before him: once, on account of the swords we wore,—and the two other times, for quarrels which the Moucres Saracens sought to have with us.

Many of us wished to purchase asses; for the camel has a very rough movement, which is extremely fatiguing to those unaccustomed to it. An ass is sold at Gaza for two ducats; but the Moucres not only wanted to prevent our buying any, but to force us to hire asses from them, at the price of five ducats to Saint Catherine's. This conduct was represented to the governor. For myself, who had hitherto rode on a camel, and had no intentions of changing, I desired they would tell me how I could ride a camel and an ass at the same time. The governor decided in our favour, and ordered that we should not be forced to hire any asses from the Moucres against our inclinations.

We here laid in fresh provision necessary for the continuation of our journey; but on the eve of our departure, four of my companions fell sick, and returned to Jerusalem. I set off with the five others, and we came to a village situated at the entrance of the desert, and the only one to be met with between Gaza and St Catherine's. Sir Sanson de Lalaing also there quitted us, and returned; so that our company consisted of sir Andrew de Toulongeon, Pierre de Vaudrei, Godefroi de Toisi, Jean de la Roe, and myself.

We thus travelled two days in the desert absolutely without seeing any thing deserving to be related. Only one morning I saw, before sun-rise, an animal running on four legs, about three feet long, but scarcely a palm in height. The Arabians fled at the sight of it, and the animal hastened to hide itself in a bush hard by. Sir Andrew and Pierre de Vaudrei dismounted, and pursued it sword in hand, when it began to cry like a cat on the approach of a dog. Pierre de Vaudrei struck it on the back with the point of his sword, but did it no harm, from its being covered with scales like a sturgeon. It sprung at sir Andrew, who, with a blow from his sword, cut the neck partly through, and flung it on its back, with its feet in the air, and killed it. The head resembled that of a large hare: the feet were like the hands of a young child, with a pretty long tail, like that of the large green lizard. Our Arabs and interpreter told us it was very dangerous *.

At the end of the second day's journey, I was seized with such a burning fever that it was impossible for me to proceed further. My four companions, distressed at this accident, made me mount an ass, and recommended me to one of our Arabs, whom they charged to reconduct me, if possible, to Gaza.

This man took a great deal of care of me, which is unusual, in respect to Christians. He faithfully kept me company, and led me in the evening to pass the night in one of their camps, which might consist of fourscore and some tents, pitched in the form of a street. These tents consist of two poles stuck in the ground by the bigger end, at a certain distance from each other, and on them is

* From this vague description, it should seem that the animal spoken of was the great lizard, called *Monitor*, because it is pretended that it gives information of the approach of a crocodile. As for the terror of the Arabs, it was groundless.

placed another pole cross-way, and over this last is laid a thick coverlid of woollen, or coarse hair.

On my arrival, four or five Arabs, who were acquainted with my companion, came to meet us. They dismounted me from my ass, and laid me on a mattress which I had with me, and then, treating me according to their method, kneaded and pinched me so much with their hands *, that from fatigue and lassitude I slept and reposed for six hours.

During all this time no one did me the least harm, nor took any thing from me. It would, however, have been very easy for them so to do; and I must have been a tempting prey, for I had with me two hundred ducats, and two camels laden with provision and wine.

I set out, on my return to Gaza, before day; but when I came thither, I found neither

* This is what is called in French ' Masser,' a method used in everal parts of the east for certain disorders.

my four companions who had remained behind nor sir Sanson de Lalaing. The whole five had returned to Jerusalem, carrying with them the interpreter. Fortunately I met with a sicilian Jew to whom I could make myself understood; and he sent me an old Samaritan, who, by some medicines which he gave me, appeased the great heat I endured.

Two days after, finding myself a little better, I set off in company with a moor, who conducted me by a road on the sea-side. We passed near to Ascalon, and thence traversed an agreeable and fertile country to Ramlé, where I regained the road to Jerusalem.

On the first day's journey, I met on my road the governor of that town, returning from a pilgrimage with a company of fifty horsemen and one hundred camels, mounted principally by women and children, who had attended him to his place of devotion. I passed the night with them, and the morrow, on my return to Jerusalem, took up my lodgings with the Cordeliers at the church of Mount Sion, where I met again my five comrades.

On my arrival, I went to bed, that my disorder might be properly treated; but I was not cured, or in a state to depart, until the 19th of August. During my convalescence, I recollected that I had frequently heard it said that it was impossible for a Christian to return overland from Jerusalem to France. I dare not, even now when I have performed this journey, assert that it is safe. I thought, nevertheless, that nothing was impossible for a man to undertake, who has a constitution, strong enough to support fatigue, and has money and health. It is not, however, through vain boasting that I say this; but, with the aid of God and his glorious mother, who never fail to assist those who pray to them heartily, I resolved to attempt the journey.

I kept my project secret for some time, without even hinting it to my companions: I was also desirous, before I undertook it, to perform other pilgrimages, especially those to Nazareth and Mount Tabor. I went, in consequence, to make Nanchardin, principal interpreter to the sultan, acquainted with my intentions, who supplied me with a sufficient interpreter for my journey. I thought of making my first pilgrimage to Mount Tabor, and every thing was prepared for it; but when I was on the point of setting out, the head of the convent where I lodged dissuaded me, and opposed my intentions most strongly. The interpreter, on his side, refused to go, saying, that in the present circumstances I would not find any person to attend me; for that the road lay through the territories of towns which were at war with each other, and that very lately a Venetian and his interpreter had been there assassinated.

I confined myself therefore to the second pilgrimage, in which sir Sanson de Lalaing and Humbert wished to accompany me. We left sir Michel de Ligne sick at Mount Sion, and his brother William remained, with his servant, to attend on him. The rest of us set off on the day of mid-August*, with the intention of going to Jaffa by way of Ramlé, and from Jaffa to Nazareth; but, before I departed, I went to the tomb of our lady, to implore her protection for my grand journey home. I heard divine service at the Cordeliers, and saw there people who call themselves Christians; 'but some of them are very strange ones, according to our manner.'

The principal monk at Jerusalem was so friendly as to accompany us as far as Jaffa, with a cordelier friar of the convent of Beaune. They there quitted us, and we engaged a bark from the Moors, which carried us to the port of Acre.

This is a handsome port, deep, and well inclosed. The town itself appears to have been large and strong; but at present there

---

* Is not this a contradiction to what he says just before?—T.

do not exist more than three hundred houses, situated at one of its extremities, and at some distance from the sea. With regard to our pilgrimage, we could not accomplish it. Some venetian merchants, whom we consulted, dissuaded us, and, from what they said, we gave it up. They told us, at the same time, that a galley from Narbonne was expected at Baruth; and my comrades being desirous to take that opportunity of returning to France, we consequently followed the road to that town.

We saw, on our way thither, Sur, an inclosed town, with a good port, then Seyde, another sea-port tolerably good. Baruth has been more considerable than it is now, but its port is still handsome, deep, and safe for vessels. On one of its points we see the remains of a strong castle which it formerly had, but which is now in ruins*.

* Sur is the ancient Tyre,—Seyde, Sidon,—Baruth, Berites. What la Brocquière here says is interesting for

As for myself, solely occupied with my grand journey, I employed the time we staid in this town in seeking information concerning it; and to this end addressed myself to a genoese merchant, called Jacques Pervézin. He advised me to go to Damascus, assuring me that I should find there merchants from Venice, Catalonia, Florence, Genoa, and elsewhere, whose counsels might guide me. He even gave me a letter of recommendation to a countryman of his, named Ottobon Escot.

Being resolved to consult Escot before I proceeded farther, I proposed to sir Sanson to go and see Damascus, without, however, telling him any thing of my project. He accepted my proposal with pleasure, and we set out under the conduct of a Moucre. I have before said that the Moucres in Syria are the

geography: it proves that all these sea-ports of Syria, formerly so commercial and famous, but at this day so degraded and completely useless, were, in his time, for the greater part, fit for commerce.

people whose trade is conducting travellers, and hiring out to them asses and mules.

On quitting Baruth, we had to traverse some high mountains to a long plain, called the valley of Noah, because it is said, that Noah there built the ark. This valley is not, at the utmost, more than a league wide; but it is pleasant and fertile, watered by two rivers, and peopled by Arabs.

As far as Damascus, we continued to travel between mountains, at whose feet are many villages and vineyards. But I warn those who, like me, shall have occasion to make this journey, to take good care of themselves during the night, for in my life I never felt such cold. This excess of cold is caused by the fall of the dew, and it is thus throughout Syria. The greater the heat during the day, the more abundant the dew, and the cold of the night.

It is two days journey from Baruth to Damascus. The Mohammedans have established a particular custom for Christians all through Syria, in not permitting them to enter the towns on horseback. None, that are known to be such, dare do it, and, in consequence, our Moucre made sir Sanson and myself dismount before we entered any town. Scarcely had we arrived in Damascus than about a dozen Saracens came round to look at us. I wore a broad beaver hat, which is unusual in that country; and one of them gave me a blow with a staff, which knocked it off my head on the ground. I own that my first movement was to lift my fist at him; but the Moucre, throwing himself between us, pushed me aside, and very fortunately for me he did so, for in an instant we were surrounded by thirty or forty persons; and if I had given a blow I know not what would have become of us.

I mention this circumstance to show that the inhabitants of Damascus are a wicked race, and, consequently, care should be taken to avoid any quarrels with them. It is the same in other mohammedan countries. I know by experience that you must not joke with them, nor at the same time seem afraid, nor appear poor, for then they will despise you; nor rich, for they are very avaricious, as all who have disembarked at Jaffa know to their cost.

Damascus may contain, as I have heard, one hundred thousand souls. The town is rich, commercial, and, after Cairo, is the most considerable of all in the possession of the sultan. To the north, south and east, is an extensive plain: to the west a mountain rises, at the foot of which the suburbs are built. A river runs through it, which is divided into several canals: the town only is inclosed by a handsome wall, for the suburbs are larger than the town. I have nowhere seen such extensive gardens, better fruits, nor greater plenty of water. This is said to be so abundant, that there is scarcely a house without a fountain.

The governor is only inferior to the sultan in all Syria and Egypt; but as at different times some governors have revolted, the sultans have taken precautions to restrain them within proper bounds. Damascus has a strong castle on the side toward the mountain, with wide and deep ditches, whereof the sultan appoints a captain of his own friends, who never suffers the governor to enter it.

It was, in 1400, destroyed, and reduced to ashes by Tamerlane. Vestiges of this disaster now remain; and toward the gate of St Paul there is a whole quarter that has never been rebuilt. There is a khan in the town, appropriated as a deposit and place of safety to merchants and their goods. It is called Khan Berkot, from its having originally been the residence of a person of that name. For my part, I believe that Berkot was a Frenchman; and what inclines me to this opinion is, that on a stone of the house are carved flowers de luce, which appear as ancient as the walls.

Whatever may have been his origin, he was a very gallant man, and to this day enjoys a high reputation in that country. Never during his lifetime, and while he was in power, could the Persians or Tartars gain the smallest portion of land in Syria. The moment he learnt that one of their armies was advancing, he instantly marched to meet it, as far as the river, beyond Aleppo, that separates Syria from Persia, and which, from a guess of the situation, I believe to be the river Jehon which falls into the Misses in Turcomania. The people of Damascus are persuaded that had he lived, Tamerlane would never have carried his arms thither. Tamerlane, however, did honour to his memory; for when he took the town, and ordered it to be set on fire, he commanded the house of Berkot to be spared, and appointed a guard to prevent its being hurt by the fire, so that it subsists to this day.

The Christians are hated at Damascus. Every evening the merchants are shut up in their houses by persons appointed for this purpose, and who, on the morrow, come to open their gates when it may please them.

I found there many genoese, venetian, calabrian, florentine, and french merchants. The last were come thither to purchase several articles, and particularly spiceries, with the intention of taking them to Baruth, and embarking them on board the galley expected from Narbonne. Among them was Jacques Coeur *, who has since acted a great part in France, and was master of the wardrobe to the king. He told us the galley was then at Alexandria, and that probably sir Andrew and

---

* Jacques Coeur was an extraordinary character, and a striking instance of the ingratitude of monarchs.

Although of low origin, he raised himself by his abilities to high honours, and acquired by his activity immense riches. He was one of the most celebrated merchants that ever existed; and had it not been for his superior management of the finances, the generals, able as they were, of Charles VII. would never have expelled the English from France.

Should time be allowed me, I shall probably publish a selection from curious papers, illustrative of his life, and of other events that took place in France during the reigns of Charles VI. Charles VII. and Louis XI.——T. J.

his three companions would embark on board at Baruth.

I was shewn the place, without the walls of Damascus, where St Paul had a vision, was struck blind, and thrown from his horse. He caused himself to be conducted to Damascus, where he was baptised; but the place of his baptism is now a mosque.

I saw also the stone from which St George mounted his horse when he went to combat the dragon. It is two feet square; and they say, that when formerly the Saracens attempted to carry it away, in spite of all the strength they employed they could not succeed.

Having seen Damascus, sir Sanson and myself returned to Baruth, where we found sir Andrew, Pierre de Vaudrei, Geoffroi de Toisi and Jean de la Roe, who had come thither, as Jacques Coeur had told us. The galley arrived from Alexandria two or three days afterward; but, during this short interval, we witnessed a feast, celebrated by the Moors in their ancient manner. It began in the evening at sun-set. Numerous companies, scattered here and there, were singing and uttering loud cries. While this was passing, the cannon of the castle were fired, and the people of the town launched into the air, ' bien hault et bien loing, une manière de feu plus gros que le plus gros fallot que je veisse oncques allumé.' They told me, they sometimes made use of such at sea, to set fire to the sails of an enemy's vessel. It seems to me, that as it is a thing easy to be made, and of little expense, it may be equally well employed to burn a camp or a thatched village, or in an engagement with cavalry to frighten the horses.

Curious to know its composition, I sent the servant of my host to the person who made this fire, and requested him to teach me the method. He returned for answer that he dared not, for that he should run great danger were it known; but as there is nothing a Moor will not do for money, I offered him a ducat, which quieted his fears, and he taught me all he knew, and even gave me the moulds in wood, with the other ingredients, which I have brought to France.

The evening before the embarkation, I took sir André de Toulongeon aside, and, having made him promise that he would not make any opposition to what I was about to reveal to him, I informed him of my design to return home overland. In consequence of his promise, he did not attempt to hinder me, but represented all the dangers I should have to encounter, and the risk I should run of being forced to deny my faith to Jesus Christ. I must own that his representations were well founded; and of all the perils he had menaced me with, there was not one I did not experience, except denying my religion. He engaged his companions to talk with me also on this subject; but what they urged was vain: I suffered them to set sail, and remained at Baruth.

On their departure, I visited a mosque that had originally been a handsome church, built, as it is said, by St Barbara. It is added, that when the Saracens had gained possession, and their criers had, as usual, ascended the tower to announce the time of prayer, they were so beaten that from that day no one has ventured to return thither.

There is also another miraculous building that has been changed into a church, which formerly was a house belonging to the Jews. One day these people finding an image of our Lord began to stone it, as their fathers had in times past stoned the Original; but the image having shed blood, they were so frightened with the miracle, that they fled and accused themselves to the bishop, and gave up even their house in reparation for their crime. A church was made from it, which at present is served by the Cordeliers.

I was lodged at the house of a venetian merchant, named Paul Barberico; and as I had no way entirely renounced my two pilgrimages to Nazareth and mount Tabor, in spite of the obstacles which it had been said I should meet with, I consulted him on this double journey. He procured for me a Moucre, who undertook to conduct me, and bound himself before him to carry me safe and sound as far as Damascus, and to bring him back from thence a certificate of having performed his engagement, signed by me. This man made me dress myself like a Saracen. The Franks, for their security in travelling, have obtained permission from the sultan to wear this dress when on a journey.

I departed with my Moucre from Baruth on the morrow after the galley had sailed, and we followed the road to Seyde that lies between the sea and the mountains. These frequently run so far into the sea that travellers are forced to go on the sands, and at other times they are three quarters of a league distant.

After an hour's ride, I came to a small wood of lofty pines, which the people of the country preserve with care. It is even forbidden to cut down any of them; but I am ignorant of the reason for such a regulation. Further on was a tolerably deep river, which my Moucre said came from the valley of Noah, but the water was not good to drink. It had a stone bridge over it, and hard by was a khan, where we passed the night.

On the morrow, we arrived at Seyde, a town situated near the sea, and inclosed on the land side by ditches, which are not deep.

Sur, called by the Moors ' Four,' has a similar situation. It is supplied with excellent water from a spring a quarter of a league to the southward of the town, conducted to it by an aqueduct. I only passed through; and it seemed to be handsome, though not strong, any more than Seyde,—both having been formerly destroyed, as appears from their walls, which are not to be compared to those of our towns.

The mountain near Sur forms a crescent, the two horns advancing as far as the sea: the void between them is not filled with villages, though there are many on the sides of the mountain. A league farther, we came to a pass which forced us to travel over a bank, on the summit of which is a tower. Travellers going to Acre have no other road than this, and the tower has been erected for their security.

From this defile to Acre, the mountains are low, and many habitations are visible, inhabited, for the greater part, by Arabs. Near the town, I met a great lord of the country, called Fancardin: he was encamped on the open plain, carrying his tents with him.

Acre, though in a plain of about four leagues in extent, is surrounded on three sides by mountains, and on the fourth by the sea. I made acquaintance there with a venetian merchant called Aubert Franc, who received me well, and procured me much useful information respecting my two pilgrimages, by which I profited. With the aid of his advice, I took the road to Nazareth, and, having crossed an extensive plain, came to the fountain, the water of which our Lord changed into wine at the marriage of Archétréclin*: it is near a village where St Peter is said to have been born.

Nazareth is another large village, built between two mountains; but the place where the angel Gabriel came to announce to the virgin Mary, that she would be a mother, is in a pitiful state. The church that had been there built is entirely destroyed; and of the house wherein our lady was when the angel appeared to her, not the smallest remnant exists.

From Nazareth I went to Mount Tabor, the place where the transfiguration of our Lord,

---

* Architriclinus is a latin word, formed from the Greek, which the evangelist applies to signify the master of the house, or major domo, who presided at the marriage of Cana. Our ignorant authors of the lower ages took it for the name of a man, and made a saint of him, whom they called Saint Archétréclin. In la Brocquière's account, Archétréclin is the bridegroom at Cana.

and many other miracles, took effect. These pasturages attract the Arabs who come thither with their beasts; and I was forced to engage four additional men as an escort, two of whom were Arabs. The ascent of the mountain is rugged, because there is no road: I performed it on the back of a mule, but it took me two hours. The summit is terminated by an almost circular plain of about two bow-shots in length, and one in width. It was formerly inclosed with walls, the ruins of which, and the ditches, are still visible: within the wall, and around it, were several churches, and one especially, where, although in ruins, full pardon for vice and sin is gained.

To the east of Mount Tabor, and at the foot of it, we saw the Tiberiade beyond which the Jordan flows: to the westward is an extensive plain, very agreeable from its gardens, filled with date palm trees, and small tufts of trees planted like vines, on which grows the cotton. At sun-rise, these last have a singular effect, and, seeing their green leaves covered with cotton, the traveller would suppose it had snowed on them *.

I descended into this plain to dinner, for I had brought with me chickens and wine. My guides conducted me to the house of a man, who, when he saw my wine, took me for a person of consequence, and received me well. He brought me a porringer of milk, another of honey, and a branch loaded with dates. They were the first I had ever seen. I noticed also the manner of manufacturing cotton, in which men and women were employed. Here my guides wanted to extort more money from me, and insisted on making a fresh bargain to reconduct me to Nazareth. I had not my sword with me, for I confess I should have drawn it; and it would have been madness

* M. de la Brocquière is here probably mistaken. The cotton tree resembles in its leaves the vine; but the cotton is formed in capsules, and not on the leaves. There are many trees, whose leaves are covered externally with a white down, but none that in this manner produce cotton.

in me, and in all who shall imitate me. The result of the quarrel was, that I was obliged to give them twelve drachms of their money, equivalent to half a ducat. The moment they had received them, the whole four left me, so that I was obliged to return alone with my Moucre.

We had not proceeded far on our road when we saw two Arabs, armed in their manner, and mounted on beautiful horses, come toward us. The Moucre was much frightened; but, fortunately, they passed us without saying a word. He owned, that had they suspected I was a Christian, they would have unmercifully killed us both, or, at the least, have stripped us naked.

Each of them bore a long and thin pole, shod at the ends with iron; one of which was pointed, the other round, but having many sharp blades a span long. Their buckler was round, according to their custom, convex at the centre, whence came a thick point of iron;

and from that point, to the bottom, it was ornamented with a long silken fringe. They were dressed in robes, whose sleeves, a foot and a half wide, hung down their arms; and, instead of a cap, they had a round hat, terminated in a point of rough crimson wool, which, instead of having the linen cloth twisted about it like other Moors, fell down, on each side of it, the whole of its breadth.

We went to lodge at Samaria, because I wished to see the lake of Tiberias, where, it is said, St Peter was accustomed to fish; and by so doing some pardons may be gained, for it was the ember-week of September. The Moucre left me to myself the whole day. Samaria is situated on the extremity of a mountain. We entered it at the close of day, and left it at midnight to visit the lake. The Moucre had proposed this hour to evade the tribute exacted from all who go thither; but the night hindered me from seeing the surrounding country.

I went first to Joseph's well, so called from his being cast into it by his brethren. There is a handsome mosque near it, which I entered, with my Moucre, pretending to be a Saracen.

Further on is a stone bridge over the Jordan, called Jacob's Bridge on account of a house hard by, said to have been the residence of that patriarch. The river flows from a great lake situated at the foot of a mountain to the north-west, on which Namcardin has a very handsome castle.

From the lake, I took the road to Damascus. The country is tolerably pleasant; and although the road leads between mountains, they are generally from one to two leagues asunder. There is, however, one narrow place, where the road is only wide enough for a horse to pass. The tract all around it, to the right and left, for the space of about a league in length and breadth, is covered with immense flint stones, like pebbles in a river, the greater part as big as a wine-tun. Beyond this pass is a handsome khan, surrounded by fountains and rivulets. Four or five miles from Damascus is another, the most magnificent I ever saw, seated near a small river, formed by a junction of springs rising on the spot. The nearer you approach the town, the finer is the country.

I met, near Damascus, a very black Moor, who had rode a camel from Cairo in eight days, though it is usually sixteen days journey. His camel had run away from him; but, with the assistance of my Moucre, we recovered it. These couriers have a singular saddle, on which they sit cross-legged; but the rapidity of the camel is so great, that to prevent any bad effects from the air, they have their heads and bodies tightly bandaged.

This courier was the bearer of an order from the sultan. A galley and two galliots, of the prince of Tarentum, had captured, before Tripoli in Syria, a vessel from the

Moors; and the sultan, by way of reprisal, had sent to arrest all the Catalonians and Genoese who might be found in Damascus and throughout Syria. This news, which my Moucre told me, did not alarm me: I entered boldly the town with other Saracens, because, dressed like them, I thought I had nothing to fear. This expedition had taken up seven days.

On the morrow of my arrival, I saw the caravan return from Mecca. It was said to be composed of three thousand camels, and, in fact, it was two days-and as many nights before they had all entered the town. This event was, according to custom, a great festival. The governor of Damascus, attended by the principal persons of the town, went to meet the caravan, out of respect to the Alcoran, which it bore. This is the book of law Mohammed left to his followers. It was enveloped in a silken covering, painted over with moorish inscriptions; and the camel that bore it was, in like manner, decorated all over with silk.

Four musicians, and a great number of drums and trumpets preceded this camel, and made a loud noise. In front, and around, were about thirty men,—some bearing cross-bows, others drawn swords, others small harquebuses, which they fired off every now and then*. Behind the camel followed eight old men, mounted on the swiftest camels, and near them were led their horses magnificently caparisoned and ornamented with rich saddles, according to the custom of the country. After them came a turkish lady, a relation of the grand seignior, in a litter borne by two camels with rich housings. There were many of these animals covered with cloth of gold.

The caravan was composed of Moors, Turks, Barbaresques, Tartars, Persians, and

* The author does not mention what sort of harquebuses these were; but it is remarkable, that our portable fire-arms, the invention of which is very recent in Europe, were, at that time, in use among the Mohammedans of Asia. u.32.

other sectaries of the false prophet Mohammed. These people pretend, that having once made a pilgrimage to Mecca, they cannot be damned. Of this I was assured by a renegado slave, a Bulgarian by birth, who belonged to the lady I have mentioned. He was called Hayauldoula, which signifies, in the turkish language, 'servant of God,' and pretended to have been three times at Mecca. I formed an acquaintance with him, because he spoke a little Italian, and often kept me company in the night as well as in the day.

In our conversations, I frequently questioned him about Mohammed, and where his body was interred. He told me it was at Mecca; that the shrine containing the body was in a circular chapel, open at the top, and that it was through this opening the pilgrims saw the shrine; that among them were some, who, having seen it, had their eyes thrust out, because they said, after what they had just seen, the world could no longer offer them any thing worth looking at. There were in fact, in this caravan, two persons, the one of sixteen and the other of twenty-two or twenty-three years old, who had thus made themselves blind.

Hayauldoula told me also, that it was not at Mecca where pardons for sin were granted, but at Medina, where St Abraham built a house that still remains *. The building is in the form of a cloister, of which pilgrims make the circuit.

With regard to the town, it is seated on the sea-shore. Indians, the inhabitants of Prester John's country, bring thither, in large ships, spices, and other productions of their country; and thither the Mohammedans go to purchase them. They load them on camels, and other beasts of burden, for the markets of Cairo, Damascus, and other places,

---

* Our traveller is mistaken. The tomb of Mohammed is at Medina and not at Mecca; and the house of Abraham is at Mecca, and not Medina, where pilgrims gain pardons, and where that great commerce is carried on.

as is well known. The distance from Mecca to Damascus is forty days journey across the desert. The heat is excessive; and many of the caravan were suffocated.

According to the renegado slave, the annual caravan to Medina should be composed of seven hundred thousand persons; and when this number is incomplete, God sends his angels to make it up. At the great day of judgment, Mohammed will admit into paradise as many persons as he shall please, where they will enjoy honey, milk, and women at pleasure.

As I was incessantly hearing Mohammed spoken of, I wished to know something about him; and, for this purpose, I addressed myself to a priest in Damascus, attached to the venetian consul, who often said mass in his house, confessed the merchants of that nation, and, when necessary, regulated their affairs. Having confessed myself to him, and settled my worldly concerns, I asked him if he were acquainted with the doctrines of Mohammed. He said he was, and knew all the Alcoran. I then besought him, in the best manner I could, that he would put down in writing all he knew of him, that I might present it to my lord the duke of Burgundy. He did so with pleasure; and I have brought with me his work.

My intention was to go to Bursa; and, in consequence, I was introduced to a Moor, who engaged to conduct me thither in the track of the caravan, on paying him thirty ducats and his expenses; but as I was advised to distrust the Moors, as people of bad faith, and subject to break their promises, I did not conclude the bargain. I say this for the instruction of those who may have any concerns with them, for I believe them to be such as they were described to me. Hayauldoula, on his part, procured me the acquaintance of some caramanian merchants, but I took another resolution.

In regard to the pilgrims that go to Mecca, the grand Turk has a custom peculiar to himself; at least, I am ignorant if the other mohammedan powers do the same; which is, that when the caravan leaves his states, he chooses for it a chief, whom they are bound to obey as implicitly as himself. The chief of this caravan was called Hoyarbarach: he was a native of Bursa, and one of its principal inhabitants. I caused myself to be presented to him by mine host and another person, as a man that wanted to go to that town to see a brother: they entreated him to receive me in his company, and to afford me his security. He asked if I understood Arabic, Turkish, Hebrew, the vulgar tongue, or Greek? When they replied that I did not, he answered, 'Well, what can he pretend to do?'

However, representations were made to him, that on account of the war I dared not go thither by sea, and that if he would condescend to admit me I would do as well as I could. He then consented; and, having placed his two hands on his head and touched his beard, he told me in the turkish language, that I might join his slaves; but he insisted that I should be dressed just like them.

I went immediately after this interview, with one of my friends, to the market, called the Bazar, and bought two long white robes that reached to my ancles, a complete turban, a linen girdle, a fustian pair of drawers to tuck the ends of my robe in,—two small bags, the one for my own use, the other to hang on my horse's head while feeding him with barley and straw,—a leathern spoon and salt, a carpet to sleep on,—and lastly a paletot (a sort of doublet) of a white skin, which I lined with linen cloth, and which was of service to me in the nights. I purchased also a white tarquais (a sort of quiver) complete, to which hung a sword and knives; but as to the tarquais and sword, I could only buy them privately,—for if those who have the administration of justice had known of it, the seller and myself would have run great risks.

The damascus blades are the handsomest and best of all Syria; and it is curious to observe their manner of burnishing them. This operation is performed before tempering; and they have, for this purpose, a small piece of wood, in which is fixed an iron, which they rub up and down the blade, and thus clear off all inequalities, as a plane does to wood: they then temper and polish it. This polish is so highly finished, that when any one wants to arrange his turban, he uses his sword for a looking-glass. As to its temper, it is perfect, and I have nowhere seen swords that cut so excellently.

There are made at Damascus, and in the adjoining country, mirrors of steel, that magnify objects like burning glasses. I have seen some that, when exposed to the sun, have reflected the heat so strongly as to set fire to a plank fifteen or sixteen feet distant.

I bought a small horse that turned out very well. Before my departure, I had him shod at Damascus; and thence, as far as Bursa, which is near fifty days journey, I had nothing to do with his feet, excepting one of the fore ones which was pricked by a nail, and made him lame for three weeks, so well do they shoe their horses. The shoes are light, thin, lengthened towards the heel, and thinner there than at the toe. They are not turned up, and have but four nail holes, two on each side. The nails are square, with a thick and heavy head. When a shoe is wanted, and it is necessary to work it to make it fit the hoof, it is done cold without ever putting it in the fire, which can readily be done because it is so thin. To pare the hoof, they use a pruning knife, similar to what vine-dressers trim their vines with, both in this as well as on the other side of the sea.

The horses of this country only walk and gallop; and, when purchased, those who have the best walk are preferred, as in Europe those who trot the best. They have wide nostrils, gallop well, and are excellent, costing little on the road; for they eat only at night, and then but a small quantity of barley with chopped straw. They never drink but in the afternoon; and their bridles are always left in their mouths, even when in the stable, like mules: when there, they have the two hinder legs tied, and they are intermixed all together, horses and mares. All are geldings, excepting a few kept for stallions. Should you have any business with a rich man, and call on him, he will carry you, to speak with you, to his stables, which are, consequently, kept always very cool, and very clean.

We, Europeans, prefer a stone-horse of a good breed, but the Moors esteem only mares. In that country, a great man is not ashamed to ride a mare, with its foal running after the dam. I have seen some exceedingly beautiful, sold as high as two or three hundred ducats.

They are accustomed to keep their horses very low, and never to allow them to get fat. The men of fortune carry with them, when they ride, a small drum, which they use in battle, or in skirmishes, to rally their men: it is fastened to the pummel of their saddles, and they beat on it with a piece of flat leather. I also purchased one, with spurs, and vermilion-coloured boots, which came up to my knees, according to the custom of the country.

As a mark of my gratitude to Hoyarbarach, I went to offer him a pot of green ginger, but he refused it; and it was by dint of prayers and entreaties that I prevailed on him to accept of it. I had not any other pledge for my security than what I have mentioned; but I found him full of frankness and good will, more, perhaps, than I should have found in many Christians.

God, who had protected me in the accomplishment of this journey, brought me acquainted with a Jew of Caffa, who spoke the tartar and italian languages; and I requested him to assist me in putting down in writing the names of every thing I might have occasion to want for myself and my horse, while on the road. On our arrival, the first day's journey, at Ballec, I drew out my paper to know how to ask for barley and chopped straw, which I wanted to give my horse. Ten or twelve Turks near me, observing my action, burst into laughter, and, coming nearer to examine my paper, seemed as much surprised at our writing as we are with theirs. They took a liking to me, and made every effort to teach me to speak Turkish: they were never weary of making me often repeat the same thing, and pronounced it so many different ways that I could not fail to retain it; so, when we separated, I knew how to call for every thing necessary for myself and horse.

During the stay of the caravan at Damascus, I made a pilgrimage about sixteen miles distant, to our lady of Serdenay. To arrive there, we traversed a mountain a full quarter of a mile in length, to which the gardens of Damascus extend. We then descended into a delightful valley, full of vineyards and gardens, with a handsome fountain of excellent water. Here, on a rock, has been erected a small castle, with a church of greek monks, having a portrait of the virgin painted on wood, whose head has been carried thither miraculously, but in what manner I am ignorant.

It is added, that it always sweats, and that this sweat is an oil *. All I can say is, that

* Many authors of the 13th century mention this virgin of Serdenay, that was famous during the croisades ; and they speak of this oily sweat, that had the reputation of doing miracles. These fabulous accounts of miraculous sweatings were common in Asia. Among others, that which exuded from the tomb of the bishop Nicholas, one of those saints whose existence is more than doubtful, was much vaunted. This pretended liquor of Nicholas was even an object of adoration; and we read, that in 1651, a clergyman at Paris, having received a phial of it, demanded and obtained

when I went thither I was shewn at the end of the church, behind the great altar, a niche formed in the wall, where I saw the image, *which was a flat thing*, and might be about one foot and a half high by one foot wide. I cannot say whether it is of wood or stone, for it was entirely covered with clothes. The front was closed with an iron trellis, and underneath was the vase containing the oil. A woman accosted me, and with a silver spoon moved aside the clothes, and wanted to anoint me with the sign of the cross on the forehead, the temples and breast. I believe this was a mere trick to get money: nevertheless, I do not mean to say that our lady may not have more power than this image.

I returned to Damascus, and on the evening of the departure of the caravan settled my affairs, and my conscience, as if

permission from the archbishop to expose it to the veneration of the faithful.—*Hist. de Paris*, &c. from *Le Boeuf*, t. 1. part 2. p. 557.

I had been at the point of death; but suddenly I found myself in great trouble. I have before mentioned the messenger whom the sultan had sent with orders to arrest all the genoese and catalonian merchants found within his dominions. By virtue of this order, my host, who was a Genoese, was arrested, his effects seized, and a Moor placed in his house to take care of them. I endeavoured to save all I could for him; and that the Moor might not notice it, I made him drunk. I was arrested in my turn, and carried before one of their cadies, who are considered as somewhat like our bishops, and have the office of administering justice. This cadi turned me over to another cadi, who sent me to prison with the merchants, although he knew I was not one; but this disagreeable affair had been brought on me by an interpreter who wanted to extort money from me, as he had before attempted on my first journey hither. Had it not been for Antoine Mourrouzin, the venetian consul, I must have paid a sum of money; but I remained in prison, and, in the mean time, the caravan set off.

The consul, to obtain my liberty, was forced to make intercession, conjointly with others, to the governor of Damascus, alledging that I had been arrested without cause, which the interpreter well knew. The governor sent for a Genoese, named Gentil Imperial, a merchant employed by the sultan to purchase slaves for him at Caffa. He asked me who I was, and my business at Damascus. On my replying that I was a Frenchman returning from a pilgrimage to Jerusalem, he said they had done wrong to detain me, and that I might depart when I pleased.

I set off on the morrow of the sixth of October, accompanied by a Moucre, whom I had first charged to carry my turkish dress out of the town, because a Christian is not permitted to wear a white turban there. At a short distance, a mountain rises, on which I was shewn a house, said to have been that of Cain. During the first day we travelled over mountains, but the road was good. On the second day we entered a fine country, which continued cheerful until we came to Balbeck.

My Moucre there quitted me, as I had overtaken the caravan. It was encamped near a river, on account of the great heat in these parts: the nights are nevertheless very cold, which will scarcely be believed, and the dews exceedingly heavy. I waited on Hoyarbarach, who confirmed the permission he had granted me to accompany him, and recommended it to me not to quit the caravan.

On the morrow morning, at eleven o'clock, I gave my horse water, with oats and straw, according, to the custom of our countries. This time the Turks said nothing to me; but at six o'clock in the evening, when, having given him water, I was about fastening the bag, that he might eat, they opposed it, and took off the bag; for they never suffer their horses to eat but during the night, and will not allow one to begin eating before the rest, unless when they are at grass.

The captain of the caravan had with him a mameluke of the sultan, who was a Circassian, and going to Caramania in search of a brother. This man seeing me alone, and ignorant of the language of the country, charitably wished to serve me as a companion, and took me with him; but, as he had no tent, we were often obliged to pass the nights under trees in gardens.

It was then that I was obliged to learn to sleep on the ground, to drink nothing but water, and to sit cross-legged. This posture was at first painful, but it was still more so to accustom myself to sit my horse with such very short stirrups,—and I suffered so much, that when I had dismounted, I could not remount without assistance, so sore were my hams; but after a little time, this manner seemed even more convenient than ours.

That same evening I supped with the mameluke; but we had only bread, cheese and milk. I had, when eating, a table-cloth, like the rich men of the country. These cloths are four feet in diameter, and round, having strings attached to them, so that they may be drawn up like a purse. When they are used, they are spread out; and when the meal is over, they are drawn up with all that remains within them, without their losing a crumb of bread or a raisin. But I observed, that whether their repast had been good or bad, they never failed to return thanks aloud to God.

Balbeck is a good town, well inclosed with walls, and tolerably commercial. In the center is a castle, built with very large stones. At present it contains a mosque, in which, it is said, there is a human skull, with eyes so enormous that a man may pass his head through their openings. I cannot affirm this for fact, as none but Saracens may enter the mosque.

From Balbeck we went to Hamos, and encamped on the banks of a river. It was there I observed their manner of encamping and pitching their tents. The tents are neither very high nor very large, so that one man can pitch them, and six persons may with ease repose in them during the heat. In the course of the day they lay open the lower parts, to give passage to the air, and close them in the night time. One camel can carry seven or eight with thin poles: some of them are very handsome.

As my companion, the Mameluke, and myself, had no tent, we fixed our quarters in a garden. There we were joined by two Turcomans of Satalia, returning from Mecca, who supped with us. These men, seeing me well clothed and well mounted, having a handsome sword, and well furnished tarquais, proposed to the Mameluke, as he afterwards owned when we separated, to make away with me, considering that I was but a Christian, and unworthy of being in their company. He answered, that since I had eaten bread and salt with them, it would be a great crime; that it was forbidden by their law; and that, after all, God had created the Christians as well as the Saracens.

They, however, persisted in their design; and as I testified a desire of seeing Aleppo, the most considerable town in Syria after Damascus, they pressed me to join them. I was ignorant of their intention, and accepted their offer; but I am now convinced they only wanted to cut my throat. The Mameluke forbade them to come any more near us, and by this means saved my life.

We set out from Balbeck two hours before day; and our caravan consisted of from four to five hundred persons, with six or seven hundred camels and mules; for it had great quantities of spicery. I will describe the order of its march.

The caravan has a very large drum; and the moment the chief orders the departure, three loud strokes are beaten. Every one then makes himself ready, and, when prepared, joins the file without uttering a word. Ten of our people would, in such cases, make more noise than a thousand of theirs. Thus they march in silence, unless it be at night, or that any one should sing a song celebrating the heroic deeds of their ancestors. At the break of day, two or three placed at a great distance from each other cry out, and answer one another, as is done from the towers of the mosques at the usual hours. In short, a little before and after run-rise, devout people make their customary prayers and oblations.

To perform these oblations, if they be near a rivulet, they dismount, and, with feet naked, they wash their whole bodies. Should there be no rivulet near, at the usual time for these ceremonies, they pass their hands over their bodies. The last among them washes his mouth and the opposite part, and then turns to the south, when all raise two fingers in the air, prostrate themselves, and kiss the ground thrice: they then rise up and say their prayers. They have been ordered to practise these ablutions instead of confessions. Persons of rank, to avoid failing in their performance, always carry, when they travel, leathern bottles full of water, which are suspended under the bellies of camels or horses, and are generally very handsome.

Hamos (Hems) is a good town, well inclosed with walls and ditches 'en glacis,' situated in a plain on the banks of a small river. Here terminates one end of the plain of Noah, which is said to extend as far as Persia. Tamerlane made his irruption through this plain when he took and destroyed so many cities. At the extremity of the town is a handsome castle, constructed on a height, with glacis as far as the walls.

From Hems, we went to Hama. The country is fine; but I saw few inhabitants excepting Arabs, who were rebuilding some of the ruined villages. I met with a merchant from Venice in Hama, named Laurent Souranze. He received me well, lodged me in his house, and shewed me the town and castle. It has good towers, with strong and thick walls, built, like the castle of Provins, on a rock, in which deep ditches have been cut. At one end of the town is the castle, strongly and well built on an elevation, which is fortified by ditches, and surmounted by a citadel which commands the whole; and the sides are washed by a river, said to be one of the four that flowed out of paradise. I know not if this be fact or not: all that I know is, that it runs east-south-east, and loses itself near Antioch.

Here is the greatest wheel I ever saw. It is put in motion by the river, and supplies the inhabitants, although numerous, with the necessary quantity of water. The water falls into a trough cut in the castle-rock, and thence is conducted to the town, where it flows through the streets in an aqueduct formed on great square pillars twelve feet high, and two wide. I was in want of several things to be like my fellow-travellers, of which the Mameluke having informed me, my host Laurent carried me himself to the bazar to purchase. The things wanted were small silken bonnets, in the fashion of the Turcomans, a cap to wear under them, turkish spoons, knives with their steel, a comb and case, and a leathern cup,— all of which are suspended to the sword. I likewise bought some finger-stalls to draw the bow, another tarquais complete—to save the one I had, which was very handsome—and lastly a capinat, which is a robe of fine white felt, impenetrable to the rain.

On the road I made acquaintance with some of my fellow-travellers, who, when they found out that I lodged with a Frank, came to ask me to procure them some wine. This liquor is forbidden them by their religion, and they dare not drink it before their own countrymen; but they hoped to do it without risk at the house of a Frank, and yet they were returning from Mecca! I spoke of it to my host Laurent, but he said he was afraid to comply, from the great dangers he should run were it known. I went to carry them this answer; but they had been more fortunate elsewhere, in procuring some at the house of a Greek. They proposed that I should accompany them to partake, whether from pure friendship, or to authorise them to drink wine in the presence of the Greek. This man conducted us to a small gallery where we all six seated ourselves in a circle on the floor. He first placed in the midst of us a large and handsome earthen jug, that might contain four gallons at least: he then brought for each of us a pot full of wine, which he poured into the jug, and placed beside it two earthen porringers to serve for glasses.

The first who began, drank to his companion, according to their custom; this did the same to the next, and so on the others. We drank in this manner for a long time without eating; at length, I perceived that I could no longer continue it without suffering, and begged of them, with uplifted hands, to permit me to leave off; but they grew very angry, and complained as if I had been resolved to interrupt their pleasure and do them an injury. Fortunately there was one among them more acquainted with me than the rest, and who loved me so that he called me ' Kardays,' that is to say, Brother. He offered to take my place, and to drink for me when it should be my turn. This appeased them, and, having accepted the offer, the party continued until evening, when it was necessary for us to return to the khan.

The captain of the caravan was, at the moment, seated on a bench of stone, and had before him a lighted torch It was not difficult for him to guess whence we came, and, consequently, four of our companions slipped away, and one only remained with me. I mention all this, to forewarn any persons that may travel through these countries, to avoid drinking with the natives, unless they shall wish to swallow so much as will make them fall to the ground.

The Mameluke, who was ignorant of my debauch, had, during that time, bought a goose for us both. He had just boiled it; and, for want of verjuice, had dressed it with the green leaves of the leek: I eat of it with him, and it lasted us for three days.

I should have liked to have seen Aleppo; but the caravan taking the strait road to Antioch, I was forced to give up all thoughts of it. As the caravan was not to set out for two days, the Mameluke proposed that we should ride forward, the more easily to procure lodgings. Four turkish merchants desired to be of our party, and we six travelled together.

Half a league from Hama, we came to the river, and crossed it by a bridge. It had overflowed, although there had not been any rain. Here I wished to give my horse some water; but as the bank was steep, and the river deep, had not the Mameluke come to my aid, I must inevitably have been drowned.

On the opposite side of the river is a long and vast plain, where we met six or eight Turcomans, accompanied by a woman. She wore a tarquais like them; and, on enquiring into this, I was told that the women of this nation are brave, and in time of war fight like men. It was added, and this seemed to me very extraordinary, that there are about thirty thousand women who thus bear the tarquais, and are under the dominion of a lord, named Turcgadiroly, who resides among the mountains of Armenia, on the frontiers of Persia.

The second day's journey was through a mountainous country, tolerably fertile, though ill watered; but we saw nothing but ruined houses. As we travelled, my Mameluke taught me to shoot with the bow, and made me buy finger-stalls and rings for this purpose. At length we arrived at a village that was rich in woods, vineyards and corn fields, but having no other water than what was in cisterns.

This district seemed to have been formerly inhabited by Christians; and I own it gave me great pleasure when I was told, that it had all belonged to Franks, and the ruins of churches were shewn me as a proof of it.

We fixed our quarters in this village; and it was then I first saw the habitations of the Turcomans, and women of that nation with uncovered faces. They commonly hide them under a piece of black tammy, to which those who are wealthy attach pieces of money and precious stones. The men are good archers. I saw several draw the bow, which they do sitting, and at a short distance; and this gives to their arrows great rapidity and strength.

On leaving Syria, we entered Turcomania, called by us Armenia. The capital is a very considerable town, named Antequayé by them, and by us Antioch. It was very flourishing in former times, and has still handsome walls in good repair, which inclose a large tract of ground, and even some mountains; but its houses are not more than three hundred in number. It is bounded on the south by a mountain, on the north by a great lake, beyond which is an open and fine country. The river that comes from Hama runs alongside the walls. Almost all the inhabitants are Turcomans or Arabs; and their profession is breeding cattle, such as camels, goats, cows and sheep.

The goats are, for the most part, white, and the handsomest I have ever seen, not having, like those of Syria, hanging ears; and their hair is soft, of some length, and curling. Their sheep have thick and broad tails. They also feed wild asses, which they tame: these much resemble stags in their hair, ears and head, and have, like them, cloven feet. I know not if they have the same cry, for I never heard them. They are large, handsome, and go with other beasts; but I have never seen them mounted *.

For the carriage of merchandise they use the buffalo and ox, as we do the horse. They also use them to ride on; and I have seen large herds, some carrying goods and others men.

* This animal cannot be an ass, for it has a cloven foot, which the ass has not. It may probably be a sort of antelope, or rather a buffalo.

The lord of this country was Ramedang, a rich, powerful and brave prince. For some time he was so redoubtable that the sultan was alarmed, and afraid to anger him; but, wishing to destroy him, he practised with the karman, who could more easily deceive Ramedang than any other, having given him his sister in marriage. In consequence, one day, as they were eating together, the karman arrested him and delivered him to the sultan, who put him to death, and took possession of Turcomania, giving, however, a portion of it to the karman. On leaving Antioch, I continued my road with the Mameluke, and we first crossed a mountain called Negre, on which he pointed out to me three or four handsome castles in ruins, that had belonged to the Christians. The road is good, and incessantly perfumed by the number of laurels with which the country abounds; but the descent is twice as rapid as the ascent. It finishes at the gulph of Asacs, which we call Layaste, because, in fact, it takes its name from the town of Ayas. This gulf extends itself between two mountains inland for upward of fifteen miles: its breadth may be about twelve, but I refer for this to the sea charts.

At the foot of the mountain, near the road, and close to the sea-shore, are the ruins of a strong castle, defended on the landside by a marsh, so that it could only be approached by sea, or by a narrow causeway across the marsh. It was inhabited, but the Turcomans had posted themselves hard by. They occupied one hundred and twenty tents, some of felt, others of white and blue cotton, all very handsome, and capable of containing, with ease, from fifteen to sixteen persons. These are their houses, and, as we do in ours, they perform in them all their household business except making fires.

We halted among them: they placed before us one of the table-cloths before mentioned, in which there remained fragments of bread, cheese and grapes. They then brought us a dozen of thin cakes of bread, with a large jug of curdled milk, called by them Yogort. The cakes are a foot broad, round, and thinner than wafers: they fold them up as grocers do their papers for spices, and eat them filled with the curdled milk.

A league further is a karavansera, where we lodged. These establishments consist of houses like the khans in Syria.

In the course of this day's journey, I overtook on the road an Armenian, who spoke a little Italian. Finding I was a Christian, he entered into conversation with me, and told me many things of the country, its inhabitants, and likewise of the sultan, and Ramedang, lord of Turcomania, whom I have already mentioned. He said, that this last was of a large size, very brave, and the most expert of all the Turks in handling a battle-axe and sword. His mother was a Christian, and had caused him to be baptised according to the greek ritual, to take from him the smell and odour of those who are not baptised *. But he was neither a good Christian nor a good Saracen; and when they spoke to him of the two prophets, Jesus and Mohammed, he said, ' For my part, I am for the living prophets: they will be more useful to me than dead ones.'

His territories on one side joined those of the karman, whose sister he had married, and on the other Syria, which belonged to the sultan. Every time the subjects of the latter passed through his country, he exacted tolls from them. But at length the sultan prevailed on the karman, as I have before noticed, to betray his brother-in-law to him; and at this moment he possesses all Turcomania as far as Tharsus, and even one day's journey further.— That day, accompanied by the Armenian, we

---

* The Christians of Asia were perfectly persuaded that the infidels had a disagreeable smell that was peculiar to them, and which baptism took away. This superstition will be again noticed. The baptism was, according to the greek ritual, by immersion.

once more lodged with the Turcomans, who again served us with milk. It was here I saw women make those thin cakes I spoke of. This is their manner of making them: they have a small round table, very smooth, on which they throw some flour, and mix it with water to a paste, softer than that for bread. This paste they divide into round pieces, which they flatten as much as possible with a wooden roller, of a smaller diameter than an egg, until they make them as thin as I have mentioned. During this operation, they have a convex plate of iron placed on a tripod, and heated by a gentle fire underneath, on which they spread the cake, and instantly turn it, so that they make two of their cakes sooner than a waferman can make one wafer.

I was two days traversing the country round the gulf. It is handsome, and had formerly many castles belonging to Christians, at present destroyed. Such was the one seen to the eastward before we arrived at Ayas.

The inhabitants are Turcomans, who are a handsome race, excellent archers, and living on little. Their dwellings are round, like pavilions, covered with felt. They live in the open plain, and have a chief whom they obey; but they frequently change their situation, when they carry their houses with them. In this case, they are accustomed to submit themselves to the lord on whose lands they fix, and even to assist him with their arms, should he be at war. But should they quit his domains, and pass over to those of his enemy, they serve him in his turn against the other; and they are noway thought the worse of for this, as it is their custom, and they are wanderers.

On my road, I met one of their chiefs hawking with falcons, with which he took tame geese. I was told, that he might have under his command ten thousand Turcomans. The country is favourable to the chace, but intersected by many small rivers that fall into the gulf. Wild boars are here abundant.

About the centre of the gulf is a defile formed by a rock, under which the road passes: it is not two bow-shots from the sea; and this passage was formerly defended by a castle, which made it very strong, but it is now in ruins.

On leaving this streight, we entered a fine extensive plain inhabited by Turcomans: my companion, the Armenian, pointed out to me a castle on a mountain, where were only people of his nation, and the walls of which were washed by a river called Jehon. We travelled along the banks of this river to a town called Misse-sur-Jehon, because it runs through it.

Misse, situated four days journey from Antioch, belonged to the Christians, and was a considerable city. Many churches, half destroyed, still remain: the choir of the great church is yet entire, but converted into a mosque. The bridge is of wood, the former stone one having been carried away by the floods. One half of the town is completely in ruins: the other half has preserved its walls, and about three hundred houses, filled with Turcomans.

From Misse to Adena, the country continues level and good, inhabited by Turcomans. Adena is two days journey from Misse, and I there proposed to wait for the caravan. It arrived: I went with the Mameluke, together with some others, many of whom were great merchants, to lodge near the bridge, between the river and the walls of the town; and it was there I observed the manner of the Turks saying their prayers and offering sacrifice. They no way hid themselves from my notice, but on the contrary seemed well pleased when I said my Pater noster, which seemed to them wonderful. I sometimes heard them chaunt their prayers at the beginning of the night,— when they seat themselves in a circle, and shake their bodies and heads while they sing in a very uncouth manner.

One day, they carried me with them to the stoves and baths of the town; and as I refused to bathe, for I must have undrest myself, and was afraid of showing my money, they gave me their clothes to keep. From this moment, we were much connected.

The bath-house is very high, and terminated by a dome, in which a circular opening is contrived to light the whole interior. The stoves and baths are handsome, and very clean. When the bathers come out of the water, they seat themselves on small hurdles of thin osiers, dry themselves, and comb their beards.

It was at Adena I first saw the two young men who had got their eyes thrust out at Mecca, after having seen the tomb of Mohammed.

The Turks bear well fatigue and a hard life: they are not incommoded, as I have witnessed, during the whole journey, by sleeping on the ground like animals. They are of a gay, cheerful humour, and willingly sing songs of the heroic deeds of their ancestors.

Any one, therefore, who wishes to live with them must not be grave or melancholy, but always have a smiling countenance. They are also men of probity, and charitable toward each other. I have often observed, that should a poor person pass by when they are eating, they would invite him to partake of their meal, which is a thing we never do.

In many places, I found they did not bake their bread half as much as ours. It is soft, and, unless a person be accustomed to it, is difficult to be chewed. In regard to meat, they eat it raw, dried in the sun. When any of their beasts, horse or camel, is so dangerously ill that no hopes remain of saving its life, they cut its throat, and eat it not raw, but a little dressed. They are very clean in the dressing their meat, but eat it dirtily. They, in like manner, keep their beard very neat and clean, but never wash their hands but when they bathe, when they are about to say their prayers, or when they wash their beards and hinder parts.

Adena is a tolerably good commercial town, well inclosed with walls, situated in a fine country, and sufficiently near the sea. The river Adena, which is wide and rises among the high mountains of Armenia, flows beneath its walls. It has over it a long bridge, and the broadest I ever saw. Its inhabitants and prince are Turcomans: the prince is brother to the brave Ramedang, whom the sultan had murdered. I was told the sultan had his son in his power, but dared not suffer him to return into Turcomania.

From Adena, I went to Thuro, which we call Tharsis. The country continues good, though near the mountains, and is inhabited by Turcomans, who live in villages or in tents. The district around Tharsis abounds in corn, wine, wood and water. It was a famous town, and very ancient buildings are still seen in it. I believe this was the town besieged by Baldwin, brother to Godfrey of Bouillon. At present it has a governor appointed by the sultan, and many Moors live within it. It is defended by a castle, with ditches 'à glacis,' and by a double wall, which in some parts is triple. A small river runs through it, and there is another at a short distance.

I found there a cypriot merchant, named Antony, who had resided in this country a long time, and knew the language well. He talked to me very pertinently about it; but he did me another favour, that of giving me some good wine, for I had not tasted any for several days.

Tharsis is but sixty miles from Curco, a castle built on the sea-shore, belonging to the king of Cyprus.

In this whole country, they speak the turkish tongue, which begins even to be spoken at Antioch, the capital, as I have before said, of Turcomania. It is a very fine language, laconic, and easily learnt.

As we had to cross the high mountains of Armenia, Hoyarbarach, the chief of our caravan would have it all assembled; and, for this purpose, he waited some days for those in the rear to come up. At last we departed, on the eve of All-souls-day. The Mameluke advised me to lay in provision for four days. I consequently purchased a sufficiency of bread and cheese for myself, and of oats and barley for my horse. On quitting Tharsis, we travelled three french leagues over a fine champaign country, peopled with Turcomans; and then we entered on the mountains, which are the highest I have ever seen. They skirt on three sides the country I had travelled over from Antioch: the sea bounds the other on the south.

We first passed through woods during a whole day, but the road is not bad. We lodged in the evening at a narrow pass, where there seemed to have been formerly a castle. The second day's journey was not at all disagreeable, and we passed the night at a caravansera. The third, we followed the banks of a small river, and saw on the mountains an innumerable quantity of speckled partridges.

In the evening, we halted on a plain about a league in length and a quarter wide, where four great valleys met;—the one by which we had come,—another that runs northward towards the country of the lord called Turcgadirony, and towards Persia: the third runs eastward, and I know not whether this also does not lead to Persia: the last extends to the westward, and it is that which I followed, and which conducted me to the country of the karman. Each of these four has a river, and the four rivers run to this last country.

It snowed much during the night. To save my horse from the weather, I covered him with my capinat, the felt robe, which I used for a cloak; but I myself caught cold, and got that disagreeable disorder, a dysentery. Had it not been for my Mameluke, I should have been in great danger; but he assisted me, and made me instantly quit the place in which

I was. We both, therefore, set off very early, and ascended the high mountains where the castle of Cublech is situated, and is the highest I am acquainted with. It is seen two days journey off; but sometimes we turned our backs to it, by reason of the windings of the mountains, sometimes also we lost sight of it, as it was hidden by their height. No one can penetrate into the country of the karman but on foot over the mountain on which this castle is built. The pass is narrow, and in some places has been perforated by the chissel, but it is every where commanded by Cublech. This castle, the last which the Armenians lost, belongs at this day to the karman, who had it in his division after the death of Ramedang.

These mountains are covered with perpetual snow, having only a road for horses, although there are some plains scattered among them. They are dangerous on account of the Turcomans who inhabit them; but during the four days I was travelling among them, I never perceived a single dwelling.

On leaving the mountains of Armenia, to enter the country of the karman, there are still others to be crossed. On one of them is a pass, having a castle called Léve, where a toll is paid to the karman. This toll was farmed to a Greek, who, on seeing me, judged from my features that I was a Christian, and stopped me. If I had been forced to return I should have been a dead man, for I was afterward assured, that before I had gone half a league my throat would have been cut, for the caravan was at a great distance. Fortunately my Mameluke bribed the Greek, and, in consideration of two ducats that I gave him, he opened the passage.

Further on is the castle of Asers, and, beyond that the castle of a town called Araclie (Eregli.)

On descending the mountain, we entered a plain as level as the sea: then are seen some heights toward the north, which, scattered here and there, appear like so many islands in the midst of the waves. It is on this plain that Eregli is situated, a town formerly inclosed, but now in the greatest state of ruin. I found there, however, some provision; for my last four days journey from Tharsus had afforded me nothing but water. The environs of the town are covered with villages, inhabited chiefly by Turcomans.

On quitting Eregli, we met two gentlemen of the country, who appeared to be men of distinction: they shewed great friendship to the Mameluke, and carried him to regale at an adjoining village, the dwellings of which are cut out of the rock. We passed the night there, but I was forced to stay the remainder of the time in a cavern, to take care of our horses. When the Mameluke returned, he told me that these two men had asked who I was, and that in his answer he had misled them, by saying I was a Circassian, who could not speak Arabic.

From Eregli to Larande, whither our route lay, is two days journey. This town, though not inclosed, is large, commercial, and well situated. There was, in ancient times, a great and strong castle in the center of the town, the gates of which are now visible: they are of iron, and very handsome, but the walls are destroyed. There is a fine plain between these two towns; and after I left Léve I did not notice a single tree in the open country.

There were in Larande two cypriot gentlemen, the one named Lyachin Castrico, the other Léon Maschero, who both spoke very tolerable French *. They inquired of me my country, and what had brought me thither: I replied, that I was a servant of my lord of Burgundy, that I came from Jerusalem,

* The Lusignans, when kings of Cyprus, toward the end of the twelfth century, had introduced the french language into that island. It was at Cyprus, when St Louis put in there on his croisade to Egypt, that the code called 'the Assizes of Jerusalem' was drawn up and published, and which became the code of laws for the Cypriots. The french language continued to be that of the court and of well educated persons.

to Damascus, and was following the caravan. They appeared astonished that I had been suffered to pass; but when they had asked whither I was going, and I had answered, that I was on my return overland through France to my foresaid lord,—they told me it was impossible to be done, and that if I had a thousand lives, I should lose them all. In consequence, they proposed that I should return to Cyprus with them; for there were at that island two galleys that had come thither to convey back the daughter of the king, who had been betrothed in marriage to the son of my lord of Savoy*; and they doubted not but the king, from the love and respect he bore to the duke of Burgundy, would grant me a passage on board one of them. I replied, that, since God had graciously permitted that

* Louis, son to Amadæus VIII. duke of Savoy. He married in 1432 Anne de Lusignan, daughter to Jean II. king of Cyprus, deceased in the month of June, and sister to Jean III, then on the throne.

I should arrive at Larande, he would probably allow me to go further; but that, at all events, I was determined to finish my journey as I had begun it, or die in the attempt.

I asked them, in my turn, whither they were going. They said their king was just dead: that during his life there had always been a truce with the grand karman, and that the young king and his council had sent them to renew this alliance. Being curious to make acquaintance with this great prince, whom his nation reverences as we do our king, I entreated permission to accompany them, to which they consented.

I met likewise with another Cypriot at Larande, called Perrin Passerot, a merchant, who had resided some time in the country. He was from Famagousta, and had been banished from that town, because he and one of his brothers had attempted to deliver it up to the king, as it was then in the hands of the Genoese.

My Mameluke also met with five or six of his countrymen. They were young circassian slaves, who were on their way to the residence of the sultan. He was desirous to regale them on their meeting; and as he had heard there were Christians at Larande, he guessed they would not be without wine, and begged of me to procure him some. By dint of inquiry, and for half a ducat, I was enabled to purchase the half of a goat-skin full, of which I made him a present.

He shewed great joy on receiving it, and instantly went to his companions, with whom he passed the whole night drinking. He himself swallowed so much that on the morrow he was near dying on the road, but he cured himself by a method which is peculiar to them. In such cases, they have a very large bottle full of water, and as their stomach becomes empty, they drink water as long as they are able, as if they would rinse a bottle, which they throw up, and then drink of it again. He was thus employed on the road until mid-day, when he was perfectly recovered.

From Larande we went to Qulongue, called by the Greeks ' Quhonguopoly *.' These places are two days journey distant from each other. The country is fine, and well furnished with villages, but wants water, and has no trees but such as have been planted near houses for their fruit, nor any other river but that which runs near the town.

This town is considerable and commercial, defended by ditches ' en glacis,' and good walls strengthened with towers, and is the best the karman possesses. There remains a small castle: formerly there was a very strong one in the center of the town, but it has been pulled down to furnish materials to build the prince's palace.

I staid there four days, that the ambassador from Cyprus and the caravan might have time

* The copyist has written it further on *Quohongue* and *Quhongue*. I shall write it henceforward *Couhongue*.

to arrive. When the ambassador came, I asked him when he intended to wait on the karman, and repeated my request to be present, which he promised to grant. There were, however, among his slaves four greek renegadoes, one of whom was his usher at arms, who united in their efforts to dissuade him from it; but he replied, that he saw no inconvenience, and, beside, that I had shewn such eagerness to witness the ceremony, that he should take pleasure in obliging me.

He was apprised of the hour when he might make his obeisance to the prince, inform him of the object of his mission, and offer his presents; for it is an established custom in the east never to appear before a superior without bringing presents. His were six pieces of camlet of Cyprus, I know not how many ells of scarlet, forty sugar loaves, a peregrine falcon, two cross-bows, and a dozen of bolts.

Some genets were sent him to carry the presents: and he and his attendants were mounted on horses, which the great lords, who had come to the palace to attend the prince during this ceremony, had left at the gate.

The ambassador made use of one of them, but dismounted at the entrance of the palace, when we were ushered into a large hall where there might be about three hundred persons. The prince occupied the adjoining apartment, around which were arranged thirty slaves standing: he was himself in a corner, seated on a carpet on the ground, according to the custom of the country, clad in a crimson and gold cloth, with his elbow leaning on a cushion of another sort of cloth of gold. Near him was his sword, his chancellor standing in front, and, at a little distance, three men seated.

The presents were first laid before him, which he scarcely deigned to look at; then the ambassador entered, attended by an interpreter, because he did not understand the turkish language. After the usual reverences, the chancellor demanded his credential letters, which he read aloud. The ambassador then addressed the king by means of his interpreter, and said, that the king of Cyprus had sent him to salute him, and to request that he would accept the presents now before him, as a mark of his friendship.

The prince made no answer, but caused him to be seated on the ground after their manner, below the three persons before mentioned, and at some distance from the prince. He now inquired after the health of his brother the king of Cyprus, and was told that he had lost his father, and had commissioned him to renew the alliance that had subsisted between the two countries during the lifetime of the deceased, for which he was very anxious. The prince answered, that he desired it as earnestly. He then questioned the ambassador when the late king died, the age of his successor, if he were prudent, if his country was obedient; and, as to these last questions, the answer was 'Yes:' he seemed well pleased.

After these words, the ambassador was told to rise, which he did, and took leave of the prince, who did not move more at his departure than at his entrance. On leaving the palace, he found the same horses which had carried him thither; and, having mounted one of them, he was reconducted to his lodgings: but he was scarcely entered when the ushers of arms presented themselves, for in these ceremonies it is customary to give them money, and the ambassador did not neglect it.

He next went to pay his compliments to the son of the prince, to offer him presents and deliver his letters. He was seated like his father, with three persons near him; but when the ambassador made his reverence, he rose up, then reseated himself, and placed the ambassador above these three personages. As for us who accompanied him, they placed us far behind,

Having noticed a bench, I was about to seat myself on it without any ceremony; but I was pulled off, and made to bend my knees and crouch on the ground like the rest.

On our return home, an usher of arms to the son visited us, as those of the father had done, who also received some money. These people, however, are satisfied with a little.

The prince and his son, in their turn, sent the ambassador a present for his expenses, which is likewise one of their customs. The first sent fifty aspres, the second thirty. An aspre is the money of the country, and fifty are equal in value to a venetian ducat.

I saw the prince go through the town in procession on a Friday, which is a holiday to them, when he was going to say his prayers. His guards were about fifty horsemen, the greater part his slaves, and about thirty infantry, who surrounded him. He bore a sword in his belt, and had a tabolcan at the pummel of his saddle, according to the custom of the country. He and his son have been baptised in the greek manner, to take off *the bad smell;* and I was told that the son's mother was a Christian. It is thus all the grandees get themselves baptised, that they may not stink.

His territories are considerable: they begin one day's journey on this side Tharsus, and extend to the country of Amurath Bey, the other kârman I spoke of, and whom we call the Grand Turk. In this line they are, as it is said, twenty leagues wide; but they are sixteen days journey in length, as I know well from having travelled them. They extend, as they assured me, on the north-east, as far as the frontiers of Persia.

The karman possesses also a maritime coast, called the Farsats. It extends from Tharsus to Courco, which belongs to the king of Cyprus, and to a port called Zabari. This district produces the most expert sailors known, but they have revolted against him.

The karman is a handsome prince, about thirty-two years old, and married to a sister of Amurath Bey. He is well obeyed by his subjects, although I have heard people say he was very cruel, and that few days passed without some noses, feet or hands being cut off, or some one put to death. Should any man be rich, he condemns him to die that he may seize his fortune; and it is said, that the greater part of his nobles have thus perished. Eight days before my arrival, he had caused one to be torn to pieces by dogs. Two days after this execution, he had caused one of his wives to be put to death, even the mother of his eldest son, who, when I saw him, knew nothing of this murder.

The inhabitants of the country are a bad race,—thieves, cheats, and great assassins: they kill each other, and justice is so relaxed that they are never arrested for it.

I found at Couhongue Antoine Passerot, brother to Perrin Passerot whom I had seen at

Larande. They had both been accused of attempting to deliver Famagousta to the king of Cyprus, and had been banished. They had retired to the states of the karman; the one to Larande, the other to Couhongue. Antony had been unfortunate. Vice sometimes blinds people; and he had been caught with a mohammedan woman, and the king had forced him to deny his religion to escape death; but he appeared to be still a staunch Catholic. In our conversations, he told me many particulars of the country, of the character and the government of the prince, and especially as to the manner in which he had taken and delivered up Ramedang.

The karman, he said, had a brother whom he banished from the country, and who took refuge at the court of the sultan, where he found an asylum. The sultan did not dare to declare war against him, but gave him to understand, that unless he delivered Ramedang into his hands he would send his brother with troops so to do. The karman made no hesitation, and rather than fight with him committed an infamous treason in regard to his brother-in-law. Antony added, that he was weak and cowardly, although his people are the bravest in all Turkey. His real name is Imbreymbas; but he is called Karman, from his being the lord of the country.

Although he is allied to the grand Turk, having married his sister, he detests him for having taken from him a portion of the karman. He is, however, afraid to make war on him, as he is the stronger; but I am persuaded that if he saw him successfully attacked by the Europeans, he would not leave him in peace.

In traversing his country, I passed near the frontiers of another, called Gasserie, which is bounded on one side by the karman, and on the other by the high mountains of Turcomania that extend toward Tharsis and Persia. Its lord is a valiant warrior, called Gadiroly, who has under his command thirty thousand turcoman men at arms, and about one hundred thousand women as brave and as fit for combat as men.

There are four lords continually at war with each other,—Gadiroly, Quharaynich, Quaraychust, and the son of Tamerlan, who is said to govern Persia.

Antony told me, that when I quitted the mountains on the other side of Eregli, I had passed within half a day's journey of a celebrated town where the body of St Basil is interred, and spoke of it in such a manner that I had a wish to see it: but he so strongly represented that I should lose more by separating myself from the caravan, and expose myself to great risks by travelling alone, that I renounced all thoughts of it.

He owned to me, that his intentions were to accompany me to my lord the duke; for that he had no desire to become a Saracen, and that, if he had entered into any engagements on this head, it was solely to escape death. It had been ordered that he should be circumcised, and he was expecting the execution of it daily, which gave him many fears. He was a very handsome man, about thirty-six years old.

He told me also, that the natives offer up public prayers in their mosques, like as we do in our churches on Sundays, in behalf of Christian princes, and for other objects which we ask from God. Now one of the things they pray to God for is, to deliver them from the coming of such a man as Godfrey of Bouillon.

The chief of the caravan making preparations to depart, I went to take leave of the cypriot ambassadors. They had flattered themselves that I would return with them, and renewed their entreaties, assuring me that I should never complete my journey; but I persisted. It was at Couhongue that the caravan broke up. Hoyarbarach took with him only his own people, his wife, two of his children, whom he had carried with him to Mecca, one or two foreign women, and myself.

I bade adieu to my Mameluke. This good man, whose name was Mohammed, had done me innumerable services. He was very charitable, and never refused alms when asked in the name of God. It was through charity he had been so kind to me, and I must confess that without his assistance I could not have performed my journey without incurring the greatest danger; and that, had it not been for his kindness, I should often have been exposed to cold and hunger, and much embarrassed with my horse.

On taking leave of him, I was desirous of shewing my gratitude; but he would never accept of any thing except a piece of our fine european cloth to cover his head, which seemed to please him much. He told me all the occasions that had come to his knowledge, on which, if it had not been for him, I should have run risks of being assassinated, and warned me to be very circumspect in my connections with the Saracens, for that there were among them some as wicked as the Franks. I write this to recal to my reader's memory, that the person who, from his love to God, did me so many and essential kindnesses, was a man not of our faith.

The country we travelled through, on leaving Couhongue, is handsome, with tolerably good villages, but the inhabitants are wicked. Hoyarbarach forbade me to go out of my quarters when we halted, even in villages, for fear lest I should be assassinated. There is near this place a celebrated bath, to which sick persons come for a cure of their several disorders. There are the remains of many houses that formerly belonged to the knights-hospitallers of Jerusalem, with the cross of Jerusalem on them.

After three days march, we came to a small town, called Achsaray, situated at the foot of a high mountain that shelters it from the south,

The country is level, but not populous, and the natives have a bad character: I was consequently forbidden to leave my house in the evening.

I travelled the ensuing day between two high mountains, whose tops are crowned with wood. The district is well peopled, partly by the Turcomans, and consists of pasture and marsh land. I there crossed a little brook that divides this country of karman from that of the other karman possessed by Amurath Bey, called by us the Grand Turk. This division resembles the former, in being a flat country, with mountains here and there.

On our road, we passed a town with a castle, called Achanay, and further on we came to a caravansera, where we intended to pass the night, but we found there twenty-five asses. Our commander refused to enter, and preferred returning a league back to a large village, where we lodged, and found bread, cheese and milk.

From this place we went to Carassar, which took two days. Carassar, in the turkish language, signifies ' black stone.' It is the capital of the country that Amurath Bey took by force of arms. Although uninclosed, it is a place of considerable trade, and has one of the finest castles I have seen, but without any other water than what is collected in cisterns. It is seated on the summit of a high rock, so round that it might be thought to be worked with a chissel. Below it is the town, surrounding it on three sides; but both are commanded by a mountain, from the north east to the north west. The other side opens to a plain, through which runs a river. Not long ago, the Greeks had gained possession of this place, but afterward lost it by their cowardice.

They dress sheeps feet here with a cleanliness I have no where seen. I regaled myself with them the more eagerly, as I had not eaten any dressed meat since I had left Couhongue. They cook also a nice dish with green walnuts. Their manner is to peel them, cut them into two, and put them on a string: then they are besprinkled with boiled wine, which attaches itself to them, and forms a jelly like paste all around them. It is a very agreeable food, especially when a person is hungry. We were obliged to lay in a stock of bread and cheese for two days, as I was disgusted with raw meat.

Two days were employed in journeying from Carassar to Cotthay. The country is good, well watered, having no very high mountains. We traversed one end of a forest, which seemed to me only remarkable for consisting entirely of oak, taller and larger than any I had hitherto met with, having besides, like fir-trees, branches only at the top.

We took up our quarters for the night at a caravansera, distant from any habitations. We found there barley and straw in plenty, and we could the more easily have supplied our wants, as there was but a single servant to take care of them; but the owners never have any thing to fear of this kind, for at such places there is no man so bold as to take the smallest article without paying for it.

On our road was a small river, renowned for its water. Hoyarbarach went to drink of it with his women, and wished me to do the same, he himself offering me some in his leathern cup. This was the first time on the journey that he had done me this favour.

Cotthay, although pretty considerable, is without walls; but it has a handsome and large castle, composed of three forts rising one above the other, on the declivity of a hill, which has a double inclosure. This place was the residence of the son of the grand Turk.

There was a caravansera in the town, whither we went to lodge. It was already occupied by a party of Turks, and we were obliged, according to custom, to turn our horses together pell-mell. On the morrow morning, when making ready to depart,

I perceived that one of my straps had been taken, which served to fasten on my horse's crupper, my carpets and other things I carried behind me.

At first, I began to cry out with much noise and anger; but there was a turkish slave present, one belonging to the sultan's son, a man of weight and about fifty years old, who, hearing me speak the language very incorrectly, took me by the hand, and conducted me to the gate of the caravansera, when he asked me in Italian who I was? I was stupified to hear him thus speak, and replied that I was a Frank. 'Whence do you come?' 'From Damascus, in company with Hoyarbarach, and I am going to Bursa to meet one of my brothers.' 'Indeed! but you are a spy, and come to make your remarks on this country. If you were not, would you not have embarked, and returned home by sea?'

This unexpected accusation confounded me: I answered, however, that the Venetians and Genoese were carrying on so bitter a war that I was afraid to venture by sea. He asked whence I came? ' From the kingdom of France,' was my answer. ' Are you from the neighbourhood of Paris?' I replied, I was not,—and in my turn asked if he were acquainted with Paris? He said he had formerly been there with a captain, named Bernabo. ' Take my advice,' continued he: ' return to the caravansera, seek your horse, and bring him hither to me, for there are some albanian slaves, who will steal from you every thing he carries. While I am taking care of him, do you go and breakfast, and procure for yourself and your horse provision for five days, for so long will you be on the road without meeting with any.'

I followed his advice, and went to purchase provision. I breakfasted also the more heartily as I had not, for two days tasted meat, and was told that I must not expect to meet with any for five days more.

When I quitted the caravansera, I took the road to Bursa, leaving that leading to Troy on my left, between the south and west points. There were many high mountains, several of which I had to pass over. I had also two days journey through forests, after which I traversed a handsome plain in which are some villages good enough for the country. Half a day's journey from Bursa, we came to one that supplied us with meat and grapes,—which last were as fresh as in the time of vintage: this mode of preserving them is a secret they have. The Turks offered me some roast meat; but it was not half dressed, and as the meat was roasting on the spit we cut off slices. We had also some kaymack, buffalo cream; and it was so good and sweet that I eat of it till I almost burst.

Before we entered this last village, we noticed the arrival of a Turk from Bursa, who had been sent to the wife of Hoyarbarach, to announce to her the death of her father. She shewed great grief on the occasion, and I had then, for the first time, an opportunity of seeing her face uncovered. She was a most beautiful woman.

There was at this place a renegado slave, a native of Bulgaria, who through affectation of zeal, and to shew himself a good Saracen, reproached the Turks of the caravan for having allowed me to be in their company, saying it was sinful in them to do so, who were returning from the holy pilgrimage to Mecca. In consequence, they notified to me that we must separate, and I was obliged to set off for Bursa.

I departed, therefore, on the morrow, an hour before day, with the aid of God, who had hitherto conducted me. He now guided me so well, that I never asked my road more than once on the whole way.

On entering the town, I met numbers of people coming out to meet the caravan, for such is the custom. The most considerable look on it as a duty, and it constitutes a festival. Several of them, supposing I was one of the pilgrims, kissed my hands and robe. When I had entered the town, I was greatly embarrassed, for I had come to a square that had four streets opening from it, and I knew not which to take. God again pointed out to me the right one, that which leads to the bazar, where the merchants reside with their merchandize. I addressed myself to the first Christian I saw, and fortunately he happened to be one of the Espinolis of Genoa, the very person to whom Parvesin of Baruth had given me letters.

He was much surprised to see me, and conducted me to the house of a Florentine, where I was lodged, as well as my horse.

I remained there ten days, and employed that time in examining the town, being conducted by the merchants, who took great pleasure in so doing

Of all the towns in the possession of the Turks, this is the most considerable. It is of great extent, carries on considerable trade, and is situated at the foot of the north side of mount Olympus, whence flows a river which, passing through the town, divides itself into several branches, forming, as it were, a number of small towns that make it look larger than it is.

It is at Bursa that the turkish sultans are buried. There are many handsome buildings, and particularly a great number of hospitals, among which there are four, where bread, wine and meat are frequently distributed to the poor who will accept of them for the sake of God. At one of the extremities of the town, toward the west, is an handsome and vast castle, built on an eminence that may well contain a thousand houses. There is also the palace of the sultan, which they told me was a very delightful place within side, having a garden and pretty pond. The prince had at that time fifty wives; and he often, as they said, amuses himself in a boat with some of them on this piece of water.

Bursa was also the residence of Camurat, bashaw, or, as we should say, governor or lieutenant of Turkey. He is a very brave man, the most active the Turk has, and the most able to conduct any enterprise, which qualities have been the principal cause of his elevation to this lieutenancy.

I asked if he governed the country well, and if he knew how to make himself obeyed? I was told that he was obeyed and respected like Amurath himself, and had for his salary fifty thousand ducats a-year; and that, when the Turk went to war, he brought him, at his own expense, twenty thousand men; but that he had likewise his pensioners, who in this case were bound to supply him at their charges, one with a thousand men, another with two, another with three thousand, and so on with the rest.

There are in Bursa two bazars; one where all sorts of silken stuffs, rich and brilliant diamonds are sold, great quantities of pearls, and cheap cotton cloths, and a variety of other merchandise, the enumeration of which would be tiresome. In the other bazar, cotton and white soap are sold, and constitute a great article of commerce.

I saw also, in a market-house, a lamentable sight,—a public sale of Christians for slaves, both men and women. The custom is to make them sit down on benches, and he who comes to buy sees only the face, the hands, and a little of the arm of the females. I witnessed at Damascus the sale of a young black girl, of not more than fifteen or sixteen years of age: she was led along the streets quite naked, excepting the belly, the hinder parts, and a little below them.

It was at Bursa that I eat, for the first time, caviare and olive oil. This food is only fit for Greeks, and when nothing better can be had. Some days after the return of Hoyarbarach, I went to take leave of him, and to thank him for the means he had procured me of continuing my journey to this place. I found him in the bazar, seated on an elevated stone bench, with many of the principal inhabitants of the town. The merchants had accompanied me in this visit: some of them, Florentines by nation, interested themselves on behalf of a Spaniard, who, having been a slave to the sultan, found means to escape from Egypt and come to Bursa. They begged I would take him with me. I carried him at my expense as far as Constantinople, where I left him; but I am persuaded he was a renegado, and I have never heard any thing of him since.

Three Genoese had bought spices from the merchants of the caravan, and intended carrying them to Pera, near Constantinople, and on the other side of the streights which we call the streights of St George, for sale. Wishing to take the advantage of their company, I waited for their departure, and for this reason staid at Bursa, for no one can pass this streight unless he be known. In this view, they procured me a letter from the governor, which I carried with me; but it was useless, for I found means to cross with them. We set out together; but they made me, for greater security, buy a high red hat with a huvette of iron wire*, which I wore as far as Constantinople.

On leaving Bursa, we travelled northward over a plain, watered by a deep river, which, about four leagues lower down, falls into the gulph between Constantinople and Gallipoli. We had a day's journey among mountains, which wood and a clayey soil made very disagreeable. There was on the road a small tree bearing a fruit somewhat bigger than our largest cherries, and of the shape and taste of strawberries, but a little acid. It is pleasant to eat; but if a great quantity be eaten, it mounts to the head, and intoxicates. It is ripe in November and December †.

* Huvette,—a kind of ornament worn on the hat.
† From the description, it seems to be the Arbutus Andrachne.

From the summit of the mountain, the gulph of Gallipoli is visible; and, when we had descended it, we entered a valley terminated by a very large lake, round which many houses are built. It was there I first saw turkish carpets made. I passed the night in this valley, which is very fertile in rice.

On pursuing our road, we came sometimes to mountains, valleys, pasture-lands, and great forests, which would be impossible to pass without a guide, and where the horses plunge so deeply in the soil they can hardly extricate themselves. I believe, for my part, that this is the forest spoken of in the history of Godfrey of Bouillon, which he had such difficulty to traverse.

I passed the night on the further side of it, at a village within four leagues of Nicomedia, which is a large town, with a harbour for shipping. This harbour is called Lenguo, and commences at the gulph of Constantinople, and extends to the town, where it is a bow-shot in breadth. All this country is difficult to travel; but beyond Nicomedia, toward Constantinople, it is very fine, and tolerably good travelling. It is more peopled with Greeks than Turks; but these Greeks have a greater aversion to the latin Christians than the Turks themselves.

I coasted the gulph of Constantinople, and, leaving the road to Nicea, a town situated to the northward near the Black Sea, I successively lodged at a village, in ruins, inhabited solely by Greeks,—then at another, near to Scutari,—and lastly at Scutari itself, on the streight, and opposite to Pera.

The Turks guard this passage, and receive a toll from all who cross it. It has rocks that would make it easy of defence, if they were fortified. Men and horses can readily embark and disembark. My companions and I crossed in two greek vessels. The owners of my boat took me for a Turk, and paid me great honours;

but when they saw me, after landing, leave my horse at the gate of Pera to be taken care of, and inquire after a genoese merchant, named Christopher Parvesin, to whom I had letters, they suspected I was a Christian.

Two of them waited for me at the gate; and when I returned for my horse, they demanded more than I had agreed on for my passage, and wanted to cheat me. I believe they would even have struck me, had they dared: I had my sword and my good tarquais; but a genoese shoemaker, who lived hard by, coming to my aid, they were forced to retreat. I mention this as a warning to travellers, who, like me, may have any thing to do with the Greeks. All those with whom I have had any concerns have only made me more suspicious, for I have found more probity in the Turks.

These people love not the Christians of the roman persuasion, and the submission which they have since made to this church was more through self-interest than sincerity*. Therefore I have been told, that a little before I came to Constantinople, the pope, in a general council, had declared them schismatics and accursed, and had devoted them to be the slaves of slaves †.

* In 1438 John Paleologus II. came to Italy to form an union between the greek and latin churches, which took place the ensuing year at the council of Florence. But this step, as la Brocquière remarks, was, on the part of the emperor, but a political operation, dictated by interest, and without consequence. His dominions were then in so miserable a state, and himself so harrassed by the Turks, that he was anxious to procure the aid of the Latins; and it was with this hope that he had come to inveigle the pope. This epocha, of 1438, is of consequence to our travels; for it proves, since la Brocquière quotes it, that he published it posterior to that year.

† A false fact. The general council that took place a little before he came to Constantinople was that of Basil in 1431, when, far from anathematising and cursing the Greeks, it was occupied about their re-union. This pretended malediction was undoubtedly a report, which those who were against this re-union spread abroad in Constantinople; and the traveller seems to have understood it by the expression, *it was told me.*

Pera is a large town, inhabited by Greeks, Jews and Genoese: the last are masters of it, under the duke of Milan, who styles himself Lord of Pera. It has a podestat and other officers, who govern it after their manner.

A great commerce is carried on with the Turks; but the latter have a singular privilege, namely, that should any of their slaves run away, and seek an asylum in Pera, they must be given up.

The port is the handsomest of all I have seen, and I believe I may add, of any in the possession of the Christians, for the largest genoese vessels may lie alongside the quays; but as all the world knows this, I shall not say more. It, however, seems to me, that on the land side, and near the church, in the vicinity of the gate at the extremity of the haven, the place is weak.

I met at Pera an ambassador from the duke of Milan, named Sir Benedicto de

Fourlino. The duke, wanting the support of the emperor Sigismond against the Venetians, and seeing Sigismond embarrassed with the defence of his kingdom of Hungary against the Turks, had sent an embassy to Amurath, to negotiate a peace between these two princes.

Sir Benedicto, in honour of my lord of Burgundy, gave me a gracious reception. He even told me, that to do mischief to the Venetians, he had contributed to make them lose Salonica, taken from them by the Turks; and certainly in this he acted so much the worse, for I have since seen the inhabitants of that town deny JESUS CHRIST, and embrace the mohammedan religion.

There was also at Pera, a Neapolitan, called Peter of Naples, with whom I was acquainted. He said he was married in the country of Prester John, and made many efforts to induce me to go thither with him. I questioned him much respecting this country, and he told me many things which I shall here insert; but I know not whether what he said be the truth, and shall not therefore warrant any part of it *.

Two days after my arrival at Pera, I crossed the haven to Constantinople, to visit that city. It is large and spacious, having the form of a triangle: one side is bounded by the streights of St George,—another, toward the south, by the bay, which extends as far as Gallipoli, and on the north side is the port.

There are, it is said, three large towns on the earth, each inclosing seven hills,— Rome, Constantinople and Antioch. Rome is, I think, larger and more compact than Constantinople. As for Antioch, as I only saw it when passing by, I cannot speak of its size:

---

* The manner in which our traveller here announces the relation of the Neapolitan shows how little he believed it; and in this, his usual good sense does not forsake him. This recital is, in fact, but a tissue of absurd fables, and revolting marvels, undeserving to be quoted, although they may generally be found in authors of those times. We shall omit them, and let the traveller continue his narration.

its hills, however, appeared to me higher than those of the two others.

They estimate the circuit of the city of Constantinople at eighteen miles, a third of which is on the land side toward the west. It is well inclosed with walls, particularly on the land side. This extent, estimated at six miles from one angle to the other, has likewise a deep ditch, ' en glacis,' excepting for about two hundred paces at one of its extremities, near the palace called la Blaquerne. I was assured that the Turks had failed in their attempt to take the town at this weak part. Fifteen or twenty feet in front of this ditch, is a false bray of a good and high wall. At the two extremities of this line, were formerly handsome palaces which, if we may judge from their present ruins, were also very strong. I was told they had been destroyed by an emperor, when taken prisoner by the Turks and in danger of his life. The conqueror insisted on his surrendering Constantinople, and, in case of refusal, threatened to put him to death. The other replied, that he preferred death to the disgrace of afflicting Christendom by so great a loss, and that his death would be nothing in comparison. When the Turk saw he could gain nothing by this means, he offered him his liberty on condition that the square in front of St Sophia should be demolished, with the two palaces. His project was, thus to weaken the town, that he might the more easily take it. The emperor accepted his offers, the proof of which exists at this day.

Constantinople is formed of many separate parts, so that it contains several open spaces to a greater extent than those built on. The largest vessels can anchor under its walls as at Pera: it has beside a small harbour in the interior, capable of containing three or four galleys. This is situated to the southward, near a gate, where a hillock is pointed out composed of bones of the Christians, who after the conquests of Jerusalem and Acre, by

Godfrey of Bouillon, were returning by this streight. When the Greeks had ferried them over, they conducted them to this place, which is remote and secret, where they were murdered. The whole, although a very numerous body, would have thus perished, had not a page found means to re-cross to Asia, and inform them of the danger that awaited them. On this, they spread themselves on the shores of the Black Sea; and from them are said to be descended those rude Christians who inhabit that part of the country,—Circassians, Mingrelians, Ziques, Gothlans and Anangats. But as this is an old story, I know of it no more than what was told me.

The city has many handsome churches; but the most remarkable and principal is that of St Sophia, where the patriarch resides, with others of the rank of canons. It is of a circular shape, situated near the eastern point, and formed of three different parts,—one subterraneous, another above the ground, and a third over that. Formerly it was surrounded by cloisters, and was three miles, as they say, in circumference. It is now of smaller extent, and only three cloisters remain, all paved, and incrusted with squares of white marble, and ornamented with large columns of various colours*. The gates are remarkable for their breadth and height, and are of brass.

This church, they say, possesses one of the robes of our Lord,—the end of the lance that pierced his side,—the sponge that was offered him to drink from,—and the reed that was put into his hand. I can only say, that behind the choir, I was shewn the gridiron on which St Laurence was broiled,—and a large stone, in the shape of a wash-stand, on which, they say, Abraham gave the angels to eat,

---

* Two of these galleries, or porticos, called by our author cloisters, as well as the columns, still subsist. These last are formed of different materials, porphyry, granite, marble, &c.; and this is the reason why the traveller, not being a naturalist, represents them as being of various colours.

when they were going to destroy Sodom and Gomorrah.

I was curious to witness the manner of the Greeks performing divine service, and went to St Sophia on a day when the patriarch officiated. The emperor was present, accompanied by his wife, his mother, and brother, the despot of the Morea *. A mystery was represented, the subject of which was the three youths whom Nebuchadnezzar had ordered to be thrown into the fiery furnace †.

The empress, daughter to the emperor of Trebisonde, seemed very handsome; but, as I was at a distance, I wished to have a nearer view,—and I was also desirous to see how she

---

* This emperor was John Paleologus II.—his brother Demetrius, despot or prince of the Peloponesus,—his mother Irene, daughter to Constantine Dragasés, sovereign of a small country in Macedonia,—his wife Maria Comnenes, daughter to Alexis, emperor of Trebisonde.

† These devout farces were then as common in the greek church as in the latin. They were called 'Mysteries' in France; and this is the name given by our traveller to the one he saw in St Sophia.

mounted her horse; for it was thus she had come to the church, attended only by two ladies, three old men, ministers of state, and three of that species of men to whose guard the Turks entrust their wives. On coming out of St Sophia, she went into an adjoining house to dine, which obliged me to wait until she returned to her palace, and consequently to pass the whole day without eating or drinking. At length she appeared. A bench was brought forth, and placed near her horse, which was superb, and had a magnificent saddle. When she had mounted the bench, one of the old men took the long mantle she wore, passed to the opposite side of the horse, and held it in his hands extended as high as he could: during this, she put her foot in the stirrup, and bestrode the horse like a man. When she was in her seat, the old man cast the mantle over her shoulders; after which one of those long hats, with a point, so common in Greece, was given to her: it was ornamented at one of the extremities with three golden plumes, and was very becoming.

I was so near that I was ordered to fall back, and consequently had a full view of her. She wore in her ears broad and flat rings, set with several precious stones, especially rubies. She looked young and fair, and handsomer than when in church. In one word, I should not have had a fault to find with her, had she not been painted, and assuredly she had not any need of it.

The two ladies mounted their horses at the same time that she did: they were both handsome, and wore, like her, mantles and hats. The company returned to the palace of la Blaquerne.

In the front of St Sophia is a large and handsome square, surrounded with walls like a palace, where games were performed in ancient times*. I saw the brother of the

* The Greek Hippodrome,—at present the Atmeidan of the Turks.

emperor, the despot of the Morea, exercising himself there, with a score of other horsemen. Each had a bow, and they galloped along the inclosure, throwing their hats before them, which, when they had passed, they shot at; and he who with his arrow pierced his hat, or was nearest to it, was esteemed the most expert. This exercise they had adopted from the Turks, and was one of which they were endeavouring to make themselves masters.

On this side, near the point of the angle, is the beautiful church of St George, which has, fronting Turkey in Asia, a tower at the narrowest part of the streights.

On the other side, to the westward, is a very high square column, with characters traced on it, and bearing on the summit an equestrian statue of Constantine in bronze. He holds a sceptre in his left hand, with his right extended towards Turkey in Asia, and the road to Jerusalem, as if to denote that the whole of that country was under his government. Near this column are three others, placed in a line, and of one single piece, bearing three gilt horses, now at Venice *.

In the pretty church of the Pantheacrator, occupied by greek monks, who are what we should call in France Grey Franciscan Friars, I was shewn a stone or table of divers colours, which Nicodemus had caused to be cut to be placed on his tomb, and which he made use of to lay out the body of our Lord, when he took him down from the cross. During this operation, the virgin was weeping over the body; but her tears, instead of remaining on it, fell on the stone, and they are all now to be seen upon it. I at first took them for drops of wax, and touched them with my hand, and then bended down to look at them horizontally, and against the light, when they seemed to me like drops of congealed water. This is a thing

* There are four,—and now at Paris.

that may have been seen by many persons as well as myself.

In the same church are the tombs of Constantine and of St Helena, his mother, raised each about eight feet high on a column, having its summit terminated in a point, cut into four sides, in the fashion of a diamond.

It is reported that the Venetians, while in power at Constantinople, took the body of St Helena from its tomb, and carried it to Venice, where they say it is now entire. It is added, that they attempted the same thing in regard to the body of Constantine, but could not succeed; and this is probable enough, for to this day two broken parts are to be seen, where they made the attempt. The two tombs are of red jasper.

In the church of St Apostola is shewn the broken shaft of the column to which our Saviour was fastened when he was beaten with rods, by order of Pilate. This shaft, longer than the height of a man, is of the same stone with the two others that I have seen, at Rome and at Jerusalem; but this exceeds in size the other two put together.

There are likewise in the same church, in wooden coffins, many holy bodies, very entire, and any one that chooses may see them. One of them had his head cut off, and that of another saint has been given him. The Greeks, however, have not the like devotion that we have for these relics. It is the same in respect to the stone of Nicodemus and the pillar of our Lord,—which last is simply inclosed by planks, and placed upright near one of the columns on the right hand of the great entrance at the front of the church.

Among the fine churches, I shall mention one more as remarkable, namely that called La Blaquerne, from being near the imperial palace, which, although small and badly roofed, has paintings, with a pavement and incrustations of marble. I doubt not but there may be others worthy of notice, but I was unable to visit them all. The latin merchants have one situated opposite to the passage to Pera, where mass, after the roman manner, is daily said.

There are merchants from all nations in this town,—but none so powerful as the Venetians, who have a bailiff that regulates all their affairs, independent of the emperor and his officers. This privilege they have enjoyed for a long time *. It is even said, that they have twice by their galleys saved the town from the Turks; but, for my part, I believe that God has spared it, more for the holy relics it contains than for any thing else. The Turks have also an officer to superintend their commerce, who, like the venetian bailiff, is independent of the emperor: they have even the privilege, that if one of their slaves shall run away, and take refuge within the city, on their demanding him, the emperor is bound to give him up.

* Since the conquest of the east by the Latins in 1204, to which conquest the Venetians greatly contributed.

This prince must be under great subjection to the Turks, since he pays him, as I am told, a tribute of ten thousand ducats annually; and this sum is only for Constantinople, for beyond that town he possesses nothing but a castle situated three leagues to the north, and in Greece a small city called Salubria.

I was lodged with a catalonian merchant, who having told one of the officers of the palace that I was attached to my lord of Burgundy, the emperor caused me to be asked if it were true that the duke had taken the Pucelle d'Orleans, which the Greeks would scarcely believe. I told them truly how the matter had passed, at which they were greatly astonished *.

* The Pucelle having bravely fought the English and the duke of Burgundy, leagued against France, had been made prisoner in 1430, by an officer of Jean de Luxembourg, the duke's general, and, being afterward sold by Jean to the English, was burnt by them the following year. This atrocious vengeance had resounded throughout Europe. At Constantinople, public rumour had attributed it to the duke; but the Greeks would not believe that a Christian prince could

The merchants informed me, that on Candlemas-day there would be a solemn service performed in the afternoon, similar to what we perform on that day, and they conducted me thither. The emperor was at one end of the hall, seated on a cushion. The empress saw the ceremony from a window in an upper apartment. The chaplains who chaunt the service are strangely ornamented and dressed: they sing the service by heart, ' selon leurs dois.'

Some days after, they carried me to see a feast given on account of the marriage of one of the emperor's relations. There was a tournament after the manner of the country, but which appeared very strange to me.

I will describe it. In the middle of a square, they had planted, like to a quintany, a large pole, to which was fastened a plank three feet wide, and five feet long. Forty

have been capable of such an atrocity, which seemed to them, says our author, as something impossible.

cavaliers advanced to this spot, without any arms or armour whatever but a short stick. They at first amused themselves by running after each other, which lasted for about half an hour,—then from sixty to fourscore rods of Alder were brought, of the thickness and length of those we use for thatching. The bridegroom first took one, and set off full gallop toward the plank, to break it: as it shook in his hand, he broke it with ease, when shouts of joy resounded, and the instruments of music, namely nacaires, like those of the Turks, began to play. Each of the other cavaliers broke their wands in the same manner. Then the bridegroom tied two of them together, which in truth were not too strong, and broke them without being wounded *. Thus ended the feast, and

* La Brocquière must have thought these justings ridiculous, from being accustomed to our tournaments, where the knights, cased in iron, fought with swords, lances and battle-axes, and when, very frequently, men were killed, wounded, or trodden under foot by the horses. This has

every one returned to his home safe and sound. The emperor and empress had been spectators of it from a window.

My intentions were to leave Constantinople with this sir Benedict de Fourlino, who, as I have said, had been sent ambassador to the Turk by the duke of Milan. There was a gentleman named Jean Visconti, and seven other persons in his company, with ten led horses; for when a traveller passes through Greece, he must absolutely carry every necessary with him.

I departed from Constantinople the 23d January 1433, and first came to the pass of Rigory, which was formerly tolerably strong: it is formed in a valley through which runs an arm of the sea, twenty miles long. There was a tower, but the Turks have destroyed it. In this place, there remain a bridge, a causeway and a greek village. In the way to Constantinople by land, there is but this pass, and another

---

made him twice say, that in this justing with sticks no one was wounded.

lower down, still more dangerous, on a river which there discharges itself into the sea.

From Rigory I went to Thiras, inhabited also by Greeks: it has been a good town, and a pass as strong as the preceding one, from being formed in like manner by the sea. At each end of the bridge, there was a large tower; but tower and town, all have been destroyed by the Turks.

I went from Thiras to Salubria. This town, two days journey from Constantinople, is situated on the gulph, that extends from this place as far as Gallipoli, and has a small harbour. The Turks could never take it, although it is not strong toward the sea. It belongs to the emperor, as well as the whole country hitherto; but this country is completely ruined, and has but poor villages.

Thence I came to Chorleu, formerly considerable,—destroyed by the Turks, and now inhabited by them and Greeks.—Next to Chorleu is Misterio, a small inclosed place, inhabited only by Greeks,—with one single Turk, to whom his prince has given it.

From Misterio we came to Pirgasy, where there are none but Turks. The walls have been thrown down.—Zambry is the next place to Pirgasy, and is equally destroyed.

We next came to Adrianople, a large commercial town, very populous, and situated on a great river called the Mariza, six days journey from Constantinople. This is the strongest town possessed by the Turk in Greece, and here he chiefly resides. The lieutenant or governor of Greece lives here also; and many merchants from Venice, Catalonia, Genoa and Florence are likewise residents. The country from Constantinople hither is good, and well watered,—but thinly peopled, having fertile vallies that produce every thing but wood.

The Turk was at Lessère *, a large town in Pyrre, near to Pharsalia, where the decisive

* Q. if not Larissa (Seres), in Phrygia.

battle was fought between Cæsar and Pompey, and sir Benedict took the road thither to wait on him. We crossed the Mariza in a boat, and shortly after met fifty women of the Turk's seraglio, attended by about sixteen eunuchs, who told us they were escorting them to Adrianople, whither their master proposed soon following them.

We came to Dymodique*, a good town, inclosed with a double wall. It is defended on one side by a river, and on the other by a large and strong castle, constructed on an elevation which is almost round, and which may contain within its extent three hundred houses. In the castle is a dungeon, wherein I was told the Turk keeps his treasure.

From Demetica, we came to Ypsala †: it has been a tolerable town, but is totally destroyed. I crossed the Mariza a second time. It is two days journey from Adrianople, and

* Q. Demetica.
† Q. Cypsela.

the country throughout was marshy, and difficult for the horses.

Ayne*, beyond Ypsala, is on the sea-shore, and at the mouth of the Mariza, which at this place is full two miles wide. When Troy flourished, this was a powerful city, and had a king: at present, its lord is brother to the lord of Matelin, and tributary to the Turk.

On a circular hillock is the tomb of Polydore, the youngest of the sons of Priam. The father had sent this son, during the siege of Troy, to the king of Eno with much treasure; but, after the destruction of Troy, the king, as much through fear of the Greeks as the wish to possess this treasure, put the young prince to death.

At Eno, I crossed the Mariza in a large vessel, and came to Macri, another maritime town to the westward of the first, and inhabited by Turks and Greeks. It is near to the island of Samandra †, which belongs to the lord

* Eno. † Q. Samothraki.

of Eno, and seems to have been formerly considerable: at present, the whole of it is in ruins, excepting a part of the castle.

Caumissin, whether we came next, after having traversed a mountain, has good walls, which make it sufficiently strong, although it is small. It is situated on a brook, in a fine flat country, inclosed by mountains to the westward; and this plain extends, for five or six days journey, to Lessère.

Missy was equally strong, and well fortified; but part of its walls are thrown down, and every thing within is destroyed: it is uninhabited.

Peritoq, an ancient town, and formerly considerable, is seated on a gulph which runs inland about forty miles, beginning at Monte Santo, where are such numbers of monks. Greeks are the inhabitants, and it is defended by good walls, which have, however, many breaches in them. Thence to Lessère, the road leads over an extensive plain. It was near Lessère, they say, that the grand battle of Pharsalia was fought.

We did not proceed to this last town; for hearing the Turk was on the road, we waited for him at Yamgbatsar, a village constructed by his subjects. When he travels, his escort consists of four or five hundred horse; but as he is passionately fond of hawking, the greater part of this troop was composed of falconers and goshawk-trainers, a people that are great favourites with him; and it is said, that he keeps more than two thousand of them. Having this passion, he travels very short days journies, which are to him more an object of amusement and pleasure.

He entered Yamgbatsar in a shower of rain, having only fifty horsemen attending him and a dozen archers, his slaves, walking on foot before him. His dress was a robe of crimson velvet, lined with sable, and on his head he wore, like the Turks, a red hat: to save himself from the rain, he had thrown over this robe another, in the manner of a mantle, after the fashion of the country.

He was encamped in a pavilion which had been brought with him; for lodgings are nowhere to be met with, nor any provision, except in the large towns, so that travellers are obliged to carry all things with them. He had numbers of camels and other beasts of burden.

In the afternoon he came out of his pavilion to go to the bath, and I saw him at my ease. He was on horseback, with the same hat and crimson robe, attended by six persons on foot. I heard him speak to his attendants, and he seemed to have a deep toned voice. He is about twenty-eight or thirty years old, and is already very fat.

The ambassador sent one of his attendants to ask him, if he could have an audience, and present him the gifts he had brought. He made answer, that being now occupied with his pleasures, he would not listen to any matters of business; that, besides, his bashaws were absent; that the ambassador must wait for them, or return to Adrianople.

Sir Benedict accepted the latter proposal, and, consequently, we returned to Caumissin, whence having repassed the mountain I have spoken of, we entered a road formed between two high rocks, and through them flows a river. A strong castle, called Coloung, had been built on one of these rocks, for its defence, but it is now in ruins. The mountain is partly covered with wood, and is inhabited by a wicked race of assassins.

At length we arrived at Trajanopoly, a town built by the emperor Trajan, who did many things worthy of record. He was the son of the founder of Adrianople; and the Saracens say, that he had an ear like to that of a sheep *. This town was very large, near to

---

* Trajanopoly was not so called from having been built by Trajan, but because he died there. It existed before his time, and was named Selinunte.

the sea and the Mariza; but now nothing is seen but ruins, with a few inhabitants. A mountain rises to the east of it, and the sea lies on the south. One of its baths bears the name of Holy Water.

Further on is Vyra, an ancient castle, demolished in many places. A Greek told me the church had three hundred canons attached to it. The choir is still remaining, but the Turks have converted it into a mosque. They have also surrounded the castle with a considerable town, inhabited by them and Greeks. It is seated on a mountain, near the Mariza.

On leaving Vyra, we met the lieutenant of Greece, whom the Turk had sent for, and

---

Adrian was not the father of Trajan, but his adopted son, and, in this right, became his successor.

Adrianople was not founded by Adrian. An earthquake had ruined it, and he ordered it to be rebuilt, and gave it his name. Such errors are excusable in an author of the fifteenth century. As for the sheep's ear, he speaks of it as a saracenic fable.

he was on his road to him with a troop of one hundred and twenty horse. He is a handsome man, a native of Bulgaria, and had been the slave of his master; but as he has the talent of drinking hard, the prince gave him the government of Greece, with a revenue of fifty thousand ducats.

Demetica, on my return, appeared much larger and handsomer than I thought it the first time; and if it be true that the Turk has there deposited his treasure, he is certainly in the right to do so.

We were forced to wait eleven days in Adrianople. At length he arrived, on the first day of Lent. The mufti, who is with them what the pope is to us, went out to meet him, accompanied by the principal persons of the town, who formed a long procession. He was already near the town when they met him, but had halted to take some refreshment, and had sent forward part of his attendants. He did not make his entry until night-fall.

During my stay at Adrianople, I had the opportunity of making acquaintance with several persons who had resided at his court, and consequently knew him well, and who told me many particulars about him. In the first place, as I have seen him frequently, I shall say that he is a little, short, thick man, with the physiognomy of a Tartar. He has a broad and brown face, high cheek bones, a round beard, a great and crooked nose, with little eyes; but they say he is kind, good, generous, and willingly gives away lands and money.

His revenues are two millions and a half of ducats, including twenty-five thousand received as tribute-money*. Besides, when he raises an army, it not only costs him nothing, but he gains by it; for the troops

---

* There must be here an error of the copyist, for 25,000 ducats as tribute is too small a sum. We shall see, further on, that the despot of Servia paid annually 50,000 for himself alone.

that are brought him from Turkey in Europe, pay at Gallipoli, the comarch, which is three aspers for each man, and five for each horse. It is the same at the passage of the Danube. Whenever his soldiers go on an expedition, and make a capture of slaves, he has the right of choosing one out of every five. He is nevertheless thought not to love war, and this seems to me well founded. He has, in fact, hitherto met with such trifling resistance from Christendom that, were he to employ all his power and wealth on this object, it would be easy for him to conquer great part of it*. His

---

* The sultan mentioned here under the name of Amourat Bey, is Amurath II. one of the most celebrated of the ottoman princes. History records many of his victories, which are indeed for the most part posterior to the account of our traveller. If he did not conquer more, it was owing to having Huniade or Scanderbeg opposed to him. But his glory was eclipsed by that of his son, the famous Mohammed II. the terror of Christians, and surnamed by his countrymen ' the great,' who twenty years after this period, in 1453, took Constantinople, and destroyed what little remained of the greek empire.

favourite pleasures are hunting and hawking; and he has, as they say, upwards of a thousand hounds, and two thousand trained hawks of different sorts, of which I have seen very many.

He loves liquor, and those who drink hard: as for himself, he can easily quaff off from ten to twelve gondils of wine, which amount to six or seven quarts *. When he has drunk much, he becomes generous, and distributes his great gifts: his attendants, therefore, are very happy when they hear him call for wine. Last year, a Moor took it into his head to preach to him on this subject, admonishing him that wine was forbidden by the prophet, and that those who drank it were not good Saracens. The only answer the prince gave was to order him to prison:

* The *quarte*, so called from being the fourth part of the chenet, which contained four pots and one french pint. The pot held two pints, consequently the quarte made two bottles more than half a septier; and twelve gondils made twenty-three bottles.

he then banished him his territories, with orders never again to set his foot on them.

He unites, to his love for women, a taste for boys, and has three hundred of the former and about thirty of the latter, which he prefers, and when they are grown up he recompenses them with rich presents and lordships. One of them he married to a sister of his, with an annual income of 25,000 ducats.

Some persons estimate his treasure at half a million of ducats, others at a million. This is exclusive of his plate, his slaves, the jewels for his women, which last article is estimated alone at a million of gold. I am convinced, that if he would for one year abstain from thus giving away blindly, and hold his hand, he would lay by a million of ducats without wronging any one.

Every now and then he makes great and remarkable examples of justice, which procures him perfect obedience at home and abroad. He likewise knows how to keep his country in an excellent state of defence, without oppressing his turkish subjects by taxes or other modes of extortion.

His houshold is composed of five thousand persons, as well horse as foot; but in war-time he does not augment their pay, so that he does not expend more than in time of peace, contrary to what happens in other nations.

His principal officers are three bashaws, or visir bashaws. The visir is a counsellor,—the bashaw a sort of chief, or lieutenant. These three have the charge of all that concerns himself or his houshold, and no one can speak with him but through them. When he is in Greece, the lieutenant of Greece has the superintendance of the army,—and when in Turkey, the lieutenant of Turkey.

He has given away great possessions, but he may resume them at pleasure. Besides, those to whom they have been given, are bound to serve him in war, with a certain number of troops, at their own expense.

It is thus that Greece annually supplies him with thirty thousand men, whom he may lead whither he pleases,—and Turkey ten thousand, for whom he only finds provisions. Should he want a more considerable army, Greece alone, as they tell me, can then furnish him with one hundred and twenty thousand more; but he is obliged to pay for these. The pay is five aspers for the infantry, and eight for the cavalry.

I have, however, heard, that of these hundred and twenty thousand, there was but half, that is to say, the cavalry, that were properly equipped, and well armed with tarquais and sword: the rest were composed of men on foot miserably accoutred,—some having swords without bows, others without swords, bows, or any arms whatever, many having only staves. It is the same with the infantry supplied by Turkey, one half armed with staves. This turkish infantry is nevertheless more esteemed than the greek, and considered as better soldiers.

Other persons, whose testimony I regard as authentic, have since told me, that the troops Turkey is obliged to furnish, when the prince wants to form an army, amount to thirty thousand men, and those from Greece to twenty, without including two or three thousand slaves of his own, whom he arms well.

Among these slaves are many Christians; and there are likewise numbers of them among the troops from Greece, Albanians, Bulgarians, and from other countries. In the last army from Greece, there were three thousand servian horse, which the despot of the province had sent under the command of one of his sons. It was with great regret that these people came to serve him, but they dared not refuse.

The bashaws arrived at Adrianople three days after their lord, bringing with them part of his people and his baggage. This baggage consists of about a hundred camels, and two hundred and fifty mules and sumpter horses, as the nation does not use waggons.

Sir Benedict was impatient to have an audience, and made inquiries of the bashaws if he could see the prince: their answer was a negative. The reason of this refusal was, that they had been drinking with him, and were all intoxicated. They, however, sent on the morrow to the ambassador to let him know they were visible, when he instantly waited on each with his presents; for such is the custom of the country, that no one can speak to them without bringing something: even the slaves who guard their gates are not exempted from it. I accompanied him on this visit.

On the following day, in the afternoon, he was informed that he might come to the palace. He instantly mounted his horse to go thither with his attendants, and I joined the company; but we were all on foot, he alone being on horseback.

In front of the court, we found a great number of men and horses. The gate was guarded by about thirty slaves, under the command of a chief, armed with staves. Should any person offer to enter without permission, they bid him retire: if he persist, they drive him away with their staves.

What we call the court of the king, the Turks call ' porte du seigneur.' Every time the prince receives a message or an embassy, which happens almost daily, ' il fait porte.' ' Faire porte,' is for him the same as when our kings of France hold royal state and open court, although there is much difference between the two ceremonies, as I shall presently show.

When the ambassador had entered, they made him sit down near the gate, with many other persons who were waiting for the prince to quit his apartment and hold his court. The three bashaws first entered, with the governor of Greece and others of the great lords. His chamber looked into a very large court: the governor went thither to wait for him.—At length he appeared. His dress was, as usual, a crimson satin robe, over which he had, by way of mantle, another of green figured satin, lined with sable. His young boys accompanied him, but no further than to the entrance of the apartment, when they returned. There was nobody with him but a small dwarf, and two young persons who acted the part of fools*.

He walked across an angle of the court to a gallery, where a seat had been prepared for him. It was a kind of couch covered with velvet, with four or five steps to mount to it. He seated himself on it, like to our taylors when they are going to work, and the three bashaws took their places a little way from him. The other officers, who on these days make part of the attendants, likewise entered the gallery, and posted themselves along the walls as far from him as they could. Without,

---

* Having fools was a very ancient custom at the eastern courts. It had been introduced by the croisaders to the courts of Christian princes, and was continued at that of France until the reign of Louis XIV.

but fronting him, were twenty wallachian gentlemen seated, who had been detained by him as hostages for the good conduct of their countrymen. Within this apartment were placed about a hundred dishes of tin, each containing a piece of mutton and rice.

When all were placed, a lord from Bosnia was introduced, who pretended that the crown of that country belonged to him, and came in consequence to do homage for it to the Turk, and ask succour from him against the present king. He was conducted to a seat near the bashaws; and when his attendants had made their appearance, the ambassador from Milan was sent for.

He advanced, followed by his presents, which were set down near the tin dishes. Persons appointed to receive them raised them above their heads, as high as they could, that the prince and his court might see them. While this was passing, sir Benedict walked slowly toward the gallery. A person of distinction came to introduce him.

On entering, he made a reverence without taking off the bonnet from his head, and when near the steps of the couch he made another very low one. The prince then rose, descended two steps to come nearer to the ambassador, and took him by the hand. The ambassador wished to kiss his hand, but he refused it; and by means of a jew interpreter, who understood the turkish and italian languages, asked how his good brother and neighbour the duke of Milan was in health. The ambassador having replied to this question, he was conducted to a seat near the Bosnian, but walking backwards, with his face toward the prince, according to the custom of the country.

The prince waited to reseat himself, until the ambassador had sitten down: then the different officers on duty who were in the apartment sat down on the floor,—and the person who had introduced the ambassador went to seek for us his attendants, and placed us near the Bosnians.

In the mean time, a silken napkin was attached to the prince, and a round piece of thin red leather was placed before him, for their usage is to eat only from table-coverings of leather, then some dressed meat was brought to him in two gilded dishes. When he was served, his officers went and took the tin dishes I have spoken of, and distributed them to the persons in the hall, one dish among four. There was in each a piece of mutton, and some clear rice, but neither bread nor any thing to drink. I saw, however, in a corner of the court a high buffet with shelves, which had some little plate on them, and at the foot was a large silver vase, in the shape of a drinking cup, which I perceived many to drink out of, but whether water or wine I know not.

With regard to the meat on the dishes, some tasted of it, others not; but before all were served, it was necessary to take away, for the prince had not been inclined to eat. He never takes any thing in public, and there are very few persons who can boast of having heard him speak, or of having seen him eat or drink.

On his going away, the musicians, who were placed in the court near the buffet, began to play. They played on instruments, and sung songs that celebrated the heroic actions of turkish warriors. When those in the gallery heard any thing that pleased them, they shouted, after their manner, most horrid cries. Being ignorant on what they were playing, I went into the court, and saw they were stringed instruments, and of a large size.

The musicians entered the apartment, and eat whatever they could find. At length the meat was taken away when every one rose up, and the ambassador retired without having said a word respecting his embassy, which is never customary at a first audience.

There is also another custom, that when an ambassador has been presented to the prince, this latter, until he shall have given him his answer, sends him wherewith to pay his daily expenses, and the sum is two hundred aspers. On the morrow, therefore, one of the officers of the treasury, the same who had conducted sir Benedict to the court, came to him with the above sum. Shortly after, the slaves who guarded the gate came for what is usually given them: they are, however, satisfied with a little.

On the third day, the bashaws let the ambassador know, they were ready to learn from him the subject of his embassy. He immediately went to the court, and I accompanied him; but the prince had closed his audience, and was just retired, and only the three bashaws, with the Beguelar or governor of Greece were now remaining. When we had passed the gate, we found these four seated on a piece of wood that happened to be withoutside of the gallery. They sent to desire the ambassador would come forward, and had a carpet placed on the ground before them, on which they made him seat himself, like to a criminal before his judge, notwithstanding there were present great numbers of people.

He explained to them the object of his mission, which was, as I heard, to entreat their lord, on the part of the duke of Milan, to consent to yield up to the roman emperor Sigismond, Hungary, Wallachia, Bulgaria as far as Sophia, Bosnia, and the part of Albania he now possessed which was dependant on Sclavonia. They replied, they could not at that moment inform the prince of his request, as he was occupied; but that within ten days he should have his answer, if they should then have received it from him. There is likewise another custom; that from the time when an ambassador is announced as such, he can never speak with the prince personally. This regulation was made since the grandfather of the present prince was murdered by an ambassador from Servia. That envoy had come to solicit from him some alleviation in favour of his countrymen, whom the prince wanted to reduce to slavery. In despair at not obtaining his object, he stabbed him, and was himself massacred the instant after *.

* The grandfather of Amurath II. was Bajazet I. who died prisoner to Tamerlane, whether treated with kindness by the conqueror, as some authors pretend, or confined in an iron cage, according to others. This story of the Servian cannot therefore regard him. But we find in the life of Amurath I. father to Bajazet, and, consequently, great grandfather to Amurath II. a circumstance that may have been the foundation for this story of the assassination.

This prince had just gained a complete victory over the despot of Servia, in which he was made prisoner, and was passing over the field of battle near to a servian soldier, mortally wounded, who, knowing him, exerted his remaining strength and poinarded him.

According to others, the despot, named Lazarus, or Eleazer Bulcowitz, finding himself attacked by Amurath, with an irresistible army, and seeing no other chance of opposing him but by treason, gains over one of the great lords of his court, who, feigning discontent, passes over to the party of

On the tenth day, we went to the court to receive the answer. The prince was there, as at the first time, seated on his couch; but he had with him in the gallery only those that served his table. I saw neither buffet, minstrels, nor the lord of Bosnia, nor the Wallachians, but only Magnoly, brother to the duke of Cephalonia, whose manners to the prince were those of a respectful servant. Even the bashaws were without, and standing at a distance, as well as the greater part of the persons whom I had before seen in the interior, but their number was much lessened.

the sultan, and assassinates him. (Du Cange Familiæ Bisant. p. 334.)

According to another account, Amurath was slain in the combat; and Lazarus, being made prisoner by the Turks, was hewed to pieces on the bleeding corpse of their master.

It seems, from the recital of la Brocquière, that the account of the assassination by the Servian, is the true one. This at least appears probable, from the precautions taken at the Ottoman Porte against foreign ambassadors; for at this day, when they are introduced to the sultan, they are held by the sleeves of their coats.

During the time we were made to wait without, the chief cadi, with his assessors, administered justice at the outward gate of the palace, when I saw some foreign Christians come to plead their cause before him: but when the prince rose up, the judges ended their sittings and retired to their homes.

I saw the prince pass with his attendants to the great court, which I was unable to do the first time. He wore a robe of cloth of gold and green, somewhat rich, and he seemed to me to have a hasty step.

When he had re-entered his apartments, the bashaws, seated as on the preceding day on the piece of wood, sent for the ambassador. Their answer was, that their master charged him to salute, in his name, his brother the duke of Milan; that he was very desirous of doing much for him, but that his present request was unreasonable; that from regard to him their prince had frequently abstained from pushing his conquests further in Hungary, which he might easily have done, and such a sacrifice ought to satisfy him; that it would be too hard for him to surrender all he had won by the sword; and that in the present circumstances, he and his soldiers had no other theatre to occupy their courage besides the territories of the emperor, and that he should be the more unwilling to renounce them, because hitherto he had never met the emperor's forces without beating them, or putting them to flight, as was well known to all the world.

The ambassador, in fact, knew this personally, for in the last defeat of Sigismond before Couloubath, he had witnessed his disaster: he had even, the night preceding the battle, quitted his camp, to wait on the Turk. In our conversations, he told me many particulars on this subject. I saw also two genoese cross-bowmen, who related to me how the emperor and his army had re-passed the Danube in his gallies.

The ambassador having received his answer from the bashaws, returned to his lodgings; but he was scarcely arrived, when he received, on the part of the sultan, five thousand aspers, with a robe of crimson camocas lined with yellow calimanco.

Thirty-six aspers are worth a venetian ducat; but of the five thousand aspers, the treasurer deducted ten per cent. as fees of office.

I saw also, during my stay at Adrianople, a present of another sort, made likewise by the sultan to a bride on her wedding day. This bride was daughter to the Begler Bey, governor of Greece; and the daughter of one of the bashaws, attended by upwards of thirty other women, had been charged to offer it. Her dress was of crimson tissue and gold: her face was covered, according to custom, with a very rich veil ornamented with diamonds. The attendant ladies had magnificent veils, and their dresses were robes of crimson velvet, and robes of cloth of gold without fur. They were all on horseback, riding astride like men, and some of them had superb saddles.

In front of the procession marched thirteen or fourteen horsemen, and two minstrels also on horseback, as well as other musicians carrying a trumpet, a very large drum, and about eight pairs of tymbals, which altogether made a most abominable noise. After the musicians came the present, and then the ladies. This present consisted of seventy broad platters of tin loaded with different sorts of sweetmeats, wet and dry, and of twenty other platters having on them sheep skinned, painted red and white, and all had a silver ring suspended from the nose, and two others in the ears.

I had an opportunity of seeing, while at Adrianople, numbers of Christians chained who were brought thither for sale. They begged for alms in the street; but my heart bleeds when I think on the shocking hardships they suffer.

We left that town on the 12th of March, under the escort of a slave whom the sultan had ordered to accompany the ambassador. This man was of great utility to us on the road, more especially in regard to lodgings,—for wherever he demanded any thing for us, it was eagerly and instantly granted.

Our first day's journey was through a beautiful country, ascending the Mariza, which we crossed at a ferry: the second, though the roads were good, was employed in passing through woods. At length, we entered Macedonia, between two mountains opening to an extensive plain, which may be forty miles wide, and is watered by the Mariza. I there met fifteen men and ten women chained by the neck, inhabitants of Bosnia, whom the Turks had just carried off in an excursion which they had made thither. Two Turks were leading them for sale to Adrianople.

Shortly after, we arrived at Philopoppoli, the capital of Macedonia, and built by king

Philip. It is situated in a plain on the Mariza, in an excellent country where all sorts of provision are sold very cheap. It was formerly a considerable town, and indeed is so now. Within it are three mountains, two of which are at one of its extremities toward the southward, and the other in the centre. On this last had been constructed a large castle, in the form of a crescent, now destroyed. I was shown the situation of king Philip's palace, which has been demolished, but the walls still remain. Philipoppoli is inhabited chiefly by Bulgarians, who follow the greek ritual.

I crossed the Mariza by a bridge, on leaving Philipoppoli, and rode a whole day over the plain I mentioned: it terminates at a mountain sixteen or twenty miles in length, covered with wood. This place was in former times infested by robbers, and very dangerous to pass. The Turk has ordered, that whoever inhabits these parts shall be free: in consequence, two villages have been erected and inhabited by Bulgarians, in one of which, situated on the confines of Bulgaria and Macedonia, I passed the night.

Having crossed the mountain, we came to a plain six miles long by two broad,—then to a forest sixteen miles in length,—then to another great plain wholly shut in by mountains, well peopled with Bulgarians, and having a river running through it.

After three days journey, I came at last to a town named Sophia, which had been very considerable, as may be judged from the ruins of its walls, now thrown down; but it is at present the best in Bulgaria. It has a small castle, and is situated near a mountain on the southward, and at the beginning of a great plain sixty miles long by ten wide. The inhabitants are chiefly Bulgarians, as in the adjacent villages. The Turks are few in number, which causes the others to feel the greatest desire to throw off their yoke, if they could find any to assist them.

I saw some Turks return from an excursion to Hungary,—and a Genoese, named Nicolas Ciba, told me he had also seen those who had crossed the Danube return, and that there was not one in ten that had both bow and sword: for my part, of those I saw, there were many more that had neither bow nor sword than those who were armed with both. The best equipped had a small wooden target. In truth, we must confess that it is a great shame for Christendom to suffer itself to be subjugated by such a race, for they are much below what is thought of them.

On quitting Sophia, I traversed fifty miles of the plain I spoke of. The country is well inhabited by Bulgarians of the greek religion. I then passed through a mountainous country, tolerably good for travelling on horseback, and came to a little town in a plain on the Nissave, called Pirotte. It is uninclosed, but has a small castle, defended on one side by the river, on the other by a marsh: to the north is a mountain. It is inhabited by Turks only.

Beyond Pirotte, the country is again mountainous, when, after a circuit, we came again to the Nissave, which runs through a beautiful valley between two tolerably high hills. At the foot of one of them was the town of Ysvouriere, now totally destroyed, even to the walls. We followed the banks of the river through the valley, and came to another mountain, difficult to pass, although cars and carts do go over it. We then arrived at an agreeable valley, still watered by the Nissave, which having crossed by a bridge, we entered Nissa.

This town had a handsome castle that belonged to the despot of Servia. The Turk took it, five years ago, by storm, and entirely destroyed it. The situation is in a delightful country, abounding in rice. I continued to follow the river from Nissa, through a country equally pleasant, and well filled with villages. I at last crossed it at a ferry, and saw it no more. The mountains now commenced, and I had a long miry forest to pass, and, after ten days journey from Adrianople, arrived at Corsebech *, a small town situated a mile distant from the Morava.

The Morava is a large river that runs from Bosnia, and divides Bulgaria from la Rascia or Servia, a province which indifferently bears these two names, and which the Turk conquered six years ago. Corsebech had a small castle, now demolished: it has still a double wall, but the upper parts, as far as the battlements, have been thrown down.

I found there Cénasnin Bey, captain or commandant of this vast frontier country, that extends from Wallachia as far as Sclavonia. He resides part of the year in this town; and

* Q. Kruzcevaz, or Alagia Hisar.

they told me he was originally a Greek, who did not drink wine like other Turks; that he was prudent and brave, and knew how to make himself feared and obeyed. The Turk has intrusted him with the government of this country, of which he possesses the greater part as his own property. He suffers no one to cross the river, unless they be known to him, or unless they be bearers of letters from his master, or, in his absence, from the governor of Greece.

We saw there a beautiful woman, one of the hungarian nobility, whose situation inspired us with pity. An hungarian renegado, one of the lowest rank, had carried her off in an excursion, and treated her as his wife. On seeing us, she melted into tears, for she had not as yet renounced her religion.

On leaving Corsebech, we crossed the Morava by a ferry, and entered the territory of the despot of Servia, a fine and well-peopled country. All on this side the river belongs to him,—the district on the other to the Turk; but the despot pays him an annual tribute of fifty thousand ducats. He possesses also, on this river, toward the common boundaries of Bulgaria, Sclavonia, Albania and Bosnia, a town called Nyeuberge, which has a mine producing gold and silver at the same time. Each year it pays him more than two hundred thousand ducats, as well informed people assured me: without this, he would be soon driven out of his dominions.

I passed on my road near to the castle of Escalache, that belongs to him. It has been a strong place, on the point of a hill, at the foot of which the Nissave forms a junction with the Morava. Part of the walls, with a tower in the form of a dungeon, are all that remain.

At the mouth of these two rivers, the Turk usually keeps from eighty to a hundred gallies, galliots and rafts, to convey over his cavalry and army in time of war. I could not see them, as no Christian is allowed to approach them; but a man, worthy of belief, informed me there was a body of three hundred men always posted there to guard them, and that they are relieved every two months.

The distance from Escalache to the Danube is one hundred miles: nevertheless, in all this distance, there does not subsist any fort, or place of defence, but a village, and a house erected by Cénasnin-Bey on the declivity of a mountain, with a mosque.

I followed the course of the Morava, and with the exception of a very miry pass, that continues about a mile, caused by a mountain pressing too close on the river, I had a good road through a pleasant well-peopled country. It was not the same the second day, for I had mountains, wood, and much mud to travel through. The country, notwithstanding, was as fine as a mountainous country can be. It is full of villages, and all your wants may be there supplied.

From the time we had entered Macedonia, Bulgaria and Servia, I found on our passage that the Turk every where caused proclamation to be made, that whoever was bound to join the army should hold himself in readiness to march. They told us, that those who, in obedience to this duty, fed a horse, were exempted from the tax of the comarch; that such Christians as were desirous of being excused from serving pay fifty aspers a-head; and that some are forced to join the army, but only when it requires reinforcements.

I learnt also at the court of the despot, that the Turk has divided the guard and defence of these frontier provinces among three captains; one, called Dysem Bey, has the district from the confines of Wallachia to the Black Sea; Cénasnin-Bey commands from Wallachia to the borders of Bosnia; and Isaac Bey from these frontiers as far as Sclavonia, that is to say, all beyond the Morava.

To continue the account of my journey, I shall say, that I came to a town, or rather a country-house, called Nicodem. It is here the despot has fixed his residence because the soil is good, and there are woods and rivers abounding with every thing needful for the pleasures of the chace and hawking, of which he is very fond.

He was out hawking by the river side, attended by fifty horse, three of his children, and a Turk, who had been sent by the sultan to summon him to send his contingent to the army, under the escort of one of his sons. Independently of his tribute, this is one of the conditions imposed upon him. Every time the sultan sends him his orders, he is obliged to furnish him with eight hundred or a thousand horse, under the command of his second son.

He gave the sultan one of his daughters in marriage: nevertheless, there passes not a day that he does not fear being deprived of his dominions. I have even heard say, that some wished to inspire the sultan with this idea, but that he had answered, ' I draw more from them now than if they were my own ; for in this case I should be obliged to give them to one of my slaves, and should not receive any thing.'

The troops he is now raising are said to be intended against Albania. Ten thousand have already marched thither, which was the reason he had so few with him when I saw him at Lessère; but this first army had been destroyed *.

The prince of Servia is a tall, handsome man, from fifty-eight to sixty years old: he has five children, three boys and two girls. Of the boys, one is twenty years, another sixteen, and the third fourteen; and all

It was in fact this same year, 1433, that the renowned Scanderbeg having, by a trick, regained possession of Albania, of which his ancestors were the sovereigns, commenced that sagacious war against Amurath, which covered him with glory, and tarnished the last years of the sultan.

three, like their father, have very agreeable countenances. In respect to the girls, one is married to the sultan, another to the count de Seil; but as I have not seen them, I cannot describe them *

When we met him hawking, the ambassador and myself took him by the hand, which I kissed, for such is the custom. On the morrow, we went to pay him our respects. He had a tolerably numerous court, composed of very handsome men, who wore the beard and hair long, as they are of the greek church. There were in the town a bishop and a doctor in theology, on their road to Constantinople, sent as ambassadors to the emperor, by the holy council of Basil †.

---

* This prince was named George Brancovitz or Wkovitz. Some account of him and his family is to be found in du Cange. (Familiæ Bisant. page 336.)

† This *holy* council concluded its sittings by citing to its tribunal, and deposing the pope, whilst the pope commanded it to dissolve itself, and convoked another at Ferrara. At Florence, he had undertaken to form an union of the greek and

I had employed two days in going from Corsebech to Nicodem, and from Nicodem to Belgrade half a day. There is nothing but forests, mountains and valleys to this town; but the vallies are crowded with villages, in which provision and good wines are met with.

Belgrade is in Servia, and did belong to the despot; but, four years ago, he ceded it to the king of Hungary, for fear lest he should suffer it to be taken by the Turk, as he had done Coulumbach. This was a heavy loss to Christendom. The other would be still greater, because the place is stronger, and can contain from five to six thousand horse*. Its walls

latin churches, and with this design had sent the ambassadors to the emperor. He came actually to Italy, and signed at Florence that political and simulated union before mentioned.

* My readers may perhaps be surprised that our author, when he speaks of the garrison of any strong place, particularizes only cavalry; and that, when he mentions the contingent sent by the despot to the turkish army, he specifies but horse. The reason is, that when he wrote, Europe paid no attention but to cavalry; and the infantry, badly armed, formed and equipped, was not considered of any consequence.

are washed on one side by a large river that comes from Bosnia, called the Save; and on the other it has a castle, near to which runs the Danube, and into this the Save flows. The town is built on the point formed by these two rivers.

Within its walls the ground rises; but on the land side, it is so flat that any one may march into the ditch. There is, however, a village on this side that extends from the Save to the Danube, and surrounds the town to the distance of a bow-shot. This village is inhabited by Servians, and on Easter-day I heard mass there in the sclavonic tongue. It is under obedience to the church of Rome, and its ceremonies are nothing different from ours.

The place is strong from its situation, and by art, having ditches en glacis, a double wall, well kept in repair, that follows exactly the rise and fall of the ground. It has also five forts, three on the elevated ground I spoke of, and two on the river, but these last are commanded by the preceding ones. It has likewise a small harbour that may hold from fifteen to twenty gallies, defended by towers constructed at each extremity. It is shut up by a chain from one tower to the other: at least, so it was told me, for the two shores are so distant I could not see it.

I saw on the Save six gallies and five galliots, near to the weakest of the five forts. In this are many Servians, but they are not permitted to enter the other forts. The whole five are well furnished with artillery. I particularly noticed three cannons of brass: two of them were formed of two pieces, and one of such a size, I never before saw the like*. Its mouth was forty-two inches in diameter, but it seemed short for its thickness †.

* From our author thus noticing the brass cannon, it should seem they were still rare in his time, and looked on as wonders. Louis XI. had a dozen cast, and gave them the names of the twelve peers of France.

† It was then the fashion to make pieces of artillery of an enormous size. Mohammed. II. at the siege of

The commandant of the place was sir Mathico, an arragonian knight, and he had for his lieutenant his own brother, styled my lord brother.

The Turk is in possession of the castle of Coulumbach, on the Danube, two days journey below Belgrade. He seized it from the despot, and it is, as they say, a strong place, but easily attacked with artillery; and all succour may be cut off from it, which is a great disadvantage. He there keeps a hundred light gallies, having sixteen or eighteen oars on a side to pass over to Hungary at his pleasure. The governor of this place is Cénasnin-Bey, before spoken of.

Constantinople, employed cannon cast on the spot that threw, as they say, balls of two hundred weight.

Monstrelet speaks of a gun that Louis XI. had cast at Tours, and carried afterward to Paris, that flung balls of five hundred pounds.

In 1717, prince Eugene, after his victory over the Turks, found in Belgrade a cannon twenty-five feet long, that shot balls of one hundred and ten pounds, whose charge was fifty-two pounds of powder. It was also then customary to make the balls of marble or stone, worked to fit the mouths of different cannons.

On the Danube, but in Hungary, and opposite to Belgrade, the despot has a town and castle that were given him by the emperor*, with several others, that afford him an income of fifty thousand ducats, on condition of his becoming his liege man, but he obeys the Turk more than the emperor.

Two days after my arrival at Belgrade, I saw twenty-five men, armed after the manner of the country, enter the town, whom count Mathico the governor had sent for to remain in garrison. They told me they were Germans, although they had Servians and Hungarians so near at hand; but they said, the Servians were subjects and tributaries to the Turk: of course, they could not trust them,—and as for the Hungarians, they were so much afraid of him, that should he appear, they would not dare to defend it, however great its strength. They were obliged, therefore, to

* Sigismond king of Bohemia and Hungary. It is pretended that Sigismond gave them in exchange for Belgrade.

call in strangers; and this measure became the more necessary from its being the only place in the possession of the emperor to enable him to pass and repass the Danube, in case of need.

This conversation greatly astonished me, and caused me to make some reflections on the strange subjection in which the Turk keeps Macedonia, Bulgaria, the emperor of Constantinople, the Greeks, the despot of Servia and his subjects. Such a dependance appeared to me a lamentable thing for Christendom; and, as I lived with the Turks, and became acquainted with their manner of living and fighting, and have frequented the company of sensible persons who have observed them narrowly in their great enterprizes, I am emboldened to write something concerning them, according to the best of my abilities, under correction, however, from those better informed, and to show how it may be possible to re-conquer the territories they have gained possession of, and to beat them in the field of battle.

I shall begin with what regards their persons, and say, they are a tolerably handsome race, with long beards, but of moderate size and strength. I know well that it is a common expression to say, as strong as a Turk,—nevertheless I have seen an infinity of Christians, when strength was necessary, excel them; and I myself, who am not of the strongest make, have, when circumstances required labour, found very many weaker than me.

They are diligent, willingly rise early, and live on little, being satisfied with bread badly baked, raw flesh dried in the sun, milk curdled or not, honey, cheese, grapes, fruit, herbs, and even a handful of flour, with which they make a potage sufficient to feed six or eight for a day. Should they have a horse or camel sick without hopes of recovery, they cut its throat and eat it. I have witnessed this many and many a time.

They are indifferent where they sleep, and lie on the ground.

Their dress consists of two or three robes of cotton, thrown one over the other, which fall to their feet. Over these again they wear another of felt, in the manner of a mantle, called a Capinat. This, though light, resists rain, and there are some very fine and handsome. Their boots come up to the knees, and they have large drawers, some of crimson velvet, others of silk or fustian and common stuffs. In war, or when travelling, to avoid being embarrassed by their robes, they tuck the ends into their drawers, by which they can move with greater freedom.

Their horses are good, cost little in food, gallop well and for a long time. They keep them very poor, never feeding them but at night, and then only giving them five or six handfuls of barley and double the quantity of chopped straw,—the whole put into a bag which hangs from their ears. At break of day, they bridle, clean and curry them, but never allow them to drink before mid day,— then in the afternoon every time that they find water, and in the evening when they lodge or encamp; for they always halt early, and near a river if possible. This last time they leave them bridled for an hour like mules, and then, at a fixed moment, each gives his horse provender.

During the night-time, they cover them with felt or other stuffs, and I have seen such coverings very handsome: they have the like also for their hounds, in which they are curious, and have a good breed; although with long hanging ears and tufted tails, which, however, they carry well.

All their horses are geldings: they keep some others for stallions, but so few, that I have never seen a single one. They saddle and bridle them ' à la genette.' Their saddles are commonly very rich, but hollow, having pummels before and behind, with short stirrup leathers and wide stirrups.

With regard to their accoutrements and dresses for war, I had twice an opportunity of seeing them, on the occasions of greek renegadoes, who, renouncing their own, had embraced the mohammedan religion. The Turks celebrate these events with much festivity. They dress themselves in their best arms, and traverse the town with as numerous a procession as possible. On these occasions I have seen them wear very handsome coats of armour like to ours, except that the links of the mail were smaller: the vambraces were the same. In one word, they resemble those pictures that represent figures of the time of Julius Cæsar. Their armour descends almost half way down the thigh; but a piece of silken stuff is attached circularly to the bottom of it, that falls down to the calf of the leg.

On their head they wear a round white cap, half a foot high, terminated in a point. It is ornamented with plates of iron on all sides, to ward off from the face, neck and cheeks, blows of the sword, and are like the helmets in France, called Salades*. Beside this head-piece, they usually wear another over it, namely a bonnet of iron wire. There are some of these so rich and handsome that they cost from forty to fifty ducats, whereas the first are bought for one or two: although not so strong as the others, they resist the cut of a sword.

I have spoken of their saddles, in which they sit, as in an arm chair, deep sunk in them, their knees very high, and with short stirrups, a position in which they cannot support the smallest blow from a lance without being unhorsed.

The arms of those who have any fortune are a bow, a tarquais, a sword, a heavy mace with a short handle, the thick end of which is cut into many angles. This is a dangerous

* A sort of light casque then in use, which, not having vizor nor throat piece, had need of projecting plates of iron to guard the face.

weapon, when struck on the shoulders, or on an unguarded arm. I am convinced that a blow given with it on a head armed with a salade would stun a man.

Several have small wooden bucklers, with which they cover themselves well on horseback when they draw the bow. I have been assured of this by those who have long used them, as well as from having seen it myself.

Their obedience to superiors is boundless. None dare disobey, even when their lives are at hazard; and it is chiefly owing to this steady submission that such great exploits have been performed, and such vast conquests gained, as render them masters of a more extensive and considerable country than all France.

I have been assured, that whenever the Christian powers have taken up arms against them, they have always had timely information of it. In this case, the sultan has their march watched by men assigned to this purpose, and he lays wait for them with his army two or three days march from the spot where he proposes to fight them. Should he think the opportunity favourable, he falls suddenly on them; and for these occasions they have a particular kind of march, beaten on a large drum. When this signal is given, those who are to lead march quietly off, followed by the others with the same silence, without the file ever being interrupted, from the horses and men being trained to this purpose. Ten thousand Turks, on such an occasion, will make less noise than one hundred men in the Christian armies. In their ordinary marches, they only walk, but in these they always gallop; and as they are beside lightly armed, they will thus advance further from evening to day-break than in three other days,—and this is the reason why they cannot wear such complete armour as the French and Italians. They choose also no horses but such as walk fast, and gallop for a long time, while we select only those that trot well and with ease.

It is by these forced marches that they have succeeded in surprising and completely defeating the Christians in their different wars. It is thus they conquered duke John, whose soul may God pardon*! and again the emperor Sigismond so recently before Coulumbach, where sir Advis, a polish knight, perished.

Their manner of fighting varies according to circumstances. When they find a favourable opportunity for it, they divide themselves into

---

* John count of Nevers, sirnamed *sans peur*, and son to Philippe le hardi, duke of Burgundy. Sigismond having formed a league, to check the conquests of Bajazet, Charles VI. sent him a body of troops, in which were two thousand gentlemen, under the command of the count of Nevers. The Christian army was defeated at Nicopolis in 1396, and the French slain or made prisoners. See further particulars in the fourth volume of Froissart.

When Jean succeeded his father, as duke of Burgundy, he caused the duke of Orleans, brother to the king of France, to be cowardly assassinated. He was murdered in his turn by Tannegui du Châtel, an ancient servant of the duke of Orleans. These facts prove that la Brocquière was in the right, when speaking of John to pray that God would pardon him.

different troops, and thus attack many parts of an army at once. This mode is particularly used when they are among woods or mountains, from the great facility they have of uniting together again.

At other times they form ambuscades, and send out scouts well mounted to observe the enemy: if their report be, that he is not on his guard, they instantly form their plan, and take advantage of the circumstance. Should they find the army well drawn up, they curvet round it within bow-shot, and while thus prancing shoot at the men and horses, and continue this manœuvre so long that they at last throw it into disorder. If the army attempt to pursue them, they fly, and disperse each separately, even should only a fourth part of their own number be ordered against them; but it is in their flight that they are formidable, and it has been almost always then that they have defeated the Christians. In flying, they have the adroitness to shoot their arrows so very true that they scarcely ever fail to hit man or horse.

Each cavalier has also on the pummel of his saddle a tabolcan. When the chief, or any of his officers, perceives the enemy who pursues to be in disorder, he gives three strokes on this instrument: the others, on hearing it, do the same, and they are instantly formed round their chief, like so many hogs round the old one,—and then, according to circumstances, they either receive the charge of the assailants, or fall on them by troops, and attack them in different places at the same time.

In pitched battles, they employ another stratagem, which consists in throwing fire-works among the cavalry to frighten the horses: they often post in their front a great body of dromedaries and camels, which are bold and vicious: these they drive before them on the enemy's line of horse, and throw it into confusion.

Such are the modes of fighting the Turks have hitherto adopted against the Christians. I would not most assuredly wrong or depreciate them; for I must own that I have always found them, in my different connections, frank and loyal, and when it was necessary to shew courage, they have never failed to do so : but I am not the less convinced, that it would be no difficult matter, for troops well mounted and well commanded, to defeat them ; and, in regard to myself, I declare, that with one half of their numbers I should never hesitate to attack them.

Their armies, I know, commonly consist of two hundred thousand men; but the greater part are on foot, and destitute, as I before said, of tarquais, helmets, mallets or sword,—few indeed being completely armed.

They have besides among them a great number of Christians, who serve through force, Greeks, Bulgarians, Macedonians, Albanians,

Sclavonians, Wallachians, Servians, and other subjects of the despots of that country.

All these people detest the Turk, because he holds them in a severe captivity; and should they see the Christians march in force against him, and above all the French, I have not the smallest doubt but they would turn against him and do him great mischief.

The Turks are not, therefore, so terribly formidable as I have heard say. I own, however, that it will be necessary, if any attempt be made against them, to have a general well obeyed by his troops, and who would particularly listen to the advice of those acquainted with their mode of warfare. This was the fault, as I am informed, of the emperor Sigismond, when he was defeated by them at Coulumbach. Had he attended to the advice given him, he would not have been forced to raise the siege, since he had from twenty-five to thirty thousand Hungarians. Did not two hundred genoese and lombardy cross-bows alone check the enemy, overawe them, and cover his retreat, while he embarked on board the gallies that he had on the Danube,—while six thousand Wallachians, under the polish knight before mentioned, having separated and posted themselves on a small eminence, were all cut to pieces.

I speak nothing here but what I have seen myself, or heard from undoubted authority: therefore, in case any Christian prince or general may wish to attempt the conquest of Turkey in Europe, or even to penetrate further, I think I am able to give much information on this subject. I shall, however, speak according to my abilities; and should any thing escape me that may be displeasing to some of my readers, I beg they will excuse it, and pass it by, as if I had said nothing.

The monarch who should form such a project ought at first to propose to himself for his object, not glory and renown, but God, religion, and the salvation of so many souls that are in the road to perdition. He must be well assured beforehand that the regular payment of his troops is provided for,—and that he carries with him none but such as have a fair reputation, with a good will for the purpose,—and, above all, that they be not pillagers. With regard to the payment of them, I think it should depend on the holy father to see that it be regularly made; but until the moment when the army enters the turkish territory, there should be made a strict law, that no one take any thing without paying for it. No person likes to see his property stolen; and I have heard, that those who have been guilty of such things have not found themselves the better for it. I, however, refer these things to the prince and the lords of his council: I shall confine myself to speak of the sort of troops I think proper for such an attempt, and whom, if I had the choice, I should like to accompany.

I would, in the first place, select from France men at arms, archers and cross-bows, in as great numbers as possible, and of the sort mentioned above. Secondly, from England, a thousand men at arms and ten thousand archers. Thirdly, from Germany, the greatest number possible of gentlemen, with their cross-bowmen on horse and foot. Collect together from fifteen to twenty thousand archers and cross-bows of these three nations, adding thereto from two to three hundred light troops; and I will ask from God the grace to march with them, and engage they shall advance without difficulty from Belgrade to Constantinople.

They will require but light armour, as I have before observed that the turkish bow has no great strength. When near, their archers shoot true and quick; but they do not shoot nearly so far as we do. Their bows are thick and short, and their arrows thin and of no length: their iron heads are stuck into the wood, which cannot bear a great blow nor make a deep wound, even on an unarmed place. From this it will be seen, slight armour only is wanted for the troops,—that is to say, light greves for the legs and thighs, thin plate armour for the body, with helmets having wide vizor-pieces. A turkish arrow would perhaps pierce a light coat of mail, but would be turned aside by plate-armour, however thin.

I shall add, that in case of necessity our archers can make use of the arrows of the Turks, but that they cannot do the same with ours, because the notch is not sufficiently wide, and the strings of their bows, being made of sinews, are too thick.

According to my opinion, our cavalry should be armed with light sharp-headed lances, and with strong well-tempered swords. It may be also advantageous to have small battle-axes on the wrist. The infantry should have double-headed battle-axes, and a long and sharp spear, both having their hands defended with gauntlets. With regard to this last article, I own I have seen some in Germany made of boiled leather, that I consider as effectual as those of iron.

When the army shall come to an open plain, where a combat may be fought with advantage, it should be done, but then the whole should be formed into one body: the van and rear guards should be employed on the wings. The pikemen to be intermixed in the line, unless it should be preferred to post them otherwise to skirmish; but the general will be careful not thus to post the men at arms. In front of the line, and on the wings, the light troops will be scattered; and every one must be strictly forbidden, under pain of death, to pursue the runaways.

It is the policy of the Turks to have their armies twice as numerous as those of the Christians. This superiority of numbers augments their courage, and allows them to form different corps, and to make their attack on various parts at the same time. Should they once force an opening, they rush through in incredible crowds, and it is then a miracle if all be not lost.

To prevent this misfortune, the light troops should be numerously posted on the angles of the line of battle, and, by this means, keep it compact, so as not to suffer it to be broken. This manœuvre seems to me the more easily to be executed, from these light troops not being sufficiently armed to form a column, capable, by its weight, of any great impulsion. The turkish lances are worth nothing: their archers are the best troops they have, and these do not shoot so strong nor so far as ours do.

They have a more numerous cavalry; and their horses, though inferior in strength to ours, and incapable of bearing such heavy weights, gallop better, and skirmish for a longer time without losing their wind. This is an additional reason for the army always keeping in a close and good order.

When this method is constantly followed, they will be forced to combat disadvantageously, and, consequently, to risk every thing, or retreat before the army. Should this last be the case, the cavalry must be sent in pursuit, but it must always march in good order, and be ever ready to fight, and receive them well, should they turn about. With such conduct, it is noway doubtful but they must alway be defeated; and if a contrary one be followed, they will beat us, as has ever happened.

I may, perhaps, be told, that it would be disgraceful thus to remain on the defensive when in presence of the enemy; and that, living as they do on little, they would starve us, unless we quitted our intrenchment to fight with them.

I shall answer, that it is not customary for them to remain long in one place; that to-day they are at this place, to morrow a day and a half's march off: they re-appear again as suddenly as they disappeared; and that if an army be not continually on its guard, it will run great risks. The important point is, to be ever on the watch from the moment they appear in sight, and ready to mount for the combat.

Should there be any difficult passage on the line of march, as many men at arms and archers must be sent thither as the situation will allow for a combat, and they must be continually in order of battle until the whole be passed. No foragers must ever be sent out, for they would be as so many lost men; and besides they would find nothing abroad, for in war-time the Turks transport every thing into towns.

With all these precautions, the conquest of Turkey in Europe would not be a difficult enterprise,—provided, I repeat it, that the army be kept in one body, never divided, and no detachments ever sent after the enemy. Should I be asked, how I would secure provision? I answer, that Turkey and Servia have navigable rivers, and Bulgaria, Macedonia and the greek provinces are fertile.

The army advancing always thus in a mass, the Turks would be forced to retreat; and they must of necessity choose one of two extremities, as I have before said,—either to re-cross into Asia, and abandon their properties, their wives and their children, since the country is, as may be seen from my description of it, defenceless,—or risk a battle, as they have always done, when they have passed the Danube.

I conclude, therefore, that with good troops composed from the three nations I have named, French, English and Germans, success would be certain; and that, if they were sufficiently numerous, well united and commanded, they might march to Jerusalem. But I shall now return to my travels.

I crossed the Danube at Belgrade. It was at this moment exceedingly swollen, and may have been twelve miles broad. Never in the memory of man had such a flood been seen. Being unable to travel to Buda by the direct road, I went to a village called Pensey. On leaving Pensey, I came to the most level plain I ever saw, and, after being ferried over a river, arrived at the town of Beurquerel, which belongs to the despot of Servia, and where I crossed two other rivers by a bridge. From Beurquerel, I came to Verchet, belonging also to the despot:—there I crossed the Theis, a wide and deep river,—and at length I arrived at Zegedin, situated upon it.

In the whole length of this road, with the exception of two small woods inclosed by a rivulet, I did not see a single tree. The natives use, for firing, straw or reeds, collected from the banks of rivers, or from their numerous marshes. They eat, instead of bread, soft cakes,—but they have not much food.

Zegedin is a large country town, of a single street that seems about a league in length. It is in a fertile country, abounding with all sorts of provision. Many cranes and bustards are taken here, and I saw the market place full of them, but they dress and eat them in a filthy manner. The Theis abounds in fish, and I have no where seen a river that produces such large ones.

Many wild horses are brought thither for sale, and their manner of conquering and taming them is curious. I have been told that, should any one want three or four thousand, they could be procured within the town; and they are so cheap that a very good road horse may be bought for ten hungarian florins. The emperor, as I heard, had given Zegedin to a bishop. I saw this bishop, and he seemed a man of a broad conscience. The cordelier friars have a handsome church in this town, where I heard service, but it was performed a little after the hungarian mode.

From Zegedin I came to Pest, a tolerably good country town on the Danube, opposite to Buda. The country, from one town to the other, was good and level, and full of immense herds of horses, that live wild on these plains like savage animals, and hence the numbers seen at the markets of Zegedin.

I crossed the Danube at Pest, and entered Buda, seven days after my departure from Belgrade. Buda is the capital of Hungary, situated on an eminence, and larger than it is broad. To the east is the Danube, to the west a valley, to the south a palace, which commands the gate of the town: it was begun by the present emperor, and, when he shall have finished it, will be extensive and strong. On this side, but without the walls, are very handsome hot baths. There are also others along the banks of the Danube to the eastward, but these are not so good as the preceding ones. —The town is governed by Germans, as well in respect to police as commerce, and what regards the different professions. Many Jews live there who speak French well, several of them being descendants of those driven formerly from France. I found also there a merchant from Arras, called Clays Davion: he was one of those whom the emperor Sigismond had brought from France to establish manufactories in his country. Clays was a tapestry weaver*.

The environs of Buda are agreeable, and its territory fertile in all sorts of provision, especially in white wines, but they are somewhat fiery, which is attributed to the adjacent hot springs, and to the sulphur they emit. One league from the town is the body of St Paul, the hermit, which is in a perfect state of preservation.

I returned to Pest, where I also found six or eight french families, whom the emperor

* Sigismond, in his travels to France, had visited the manufactories, and particularly those of Flanders, at that time famous for its tapestries. He wished to establish similar ones in his capital of Hungary, and for this effect had engaged different workmen to follow him.

had sent thither to construct on the Danube, and opposite to his palace, a large tower. His intentions were, to shut up the river with a chain extending from it; and I should suppose he wanted to imitate what had been done from the town of Burgundy that fronts the fort of L'Ecluse; but I do not believe it is practicable here, for the river is too broad. I had the curiosity to visit the tower, which is about the length of three lances high, and round about were quantities of hewn stone; but it had remained some time in this state, because the masons who had begun the work were dead, and those that had survived them were said not to have knowledge enough to continue it.

Pest is inhabited by many horse-dealers; and whoever may want two thousand good horses, they can furnish the quantity. They sell them by stables full, containing ten horses, and their price for each stable is two hundred florins. I looked into several, where two or three horses alone were worth that price.

They come for the most part from the mountains of Transylvania, which bound Hungary to the eastward. I purchased one, that galloped well, as indeed they almost all do. The country is excellent for breeding them, from the quantity of grass it produces; but they have the fault of being a little headstrong, and particularly difficult to shoe, so that I have sometimes seen them obliged to be cast on the ground to be shod.

The mountains just spoken of contain mines of gold and salt, each of which pay annually to the king one hundred hungarian florins. He had given up that of gold to the lord of Prussia and to count Mathico, on condition that the first would guard the frontier against the Turk, and the second Belgrade. The queen had reserved to her own use the revenue from salt.

The salt is beautiful: it is cut out of a rock like free stone, into pieces of about a foot long, squared, but a little convex on the upper side. Whoever should see them in a cart would take them for stone. It is afterward pounded in a mortar, and turns out tolerably white, but finer and better than any I have elsewhere tasted.

In my road through Hungary, I have frequently met waggons with six, seven or eight persons in them, and drawn by only a single horse; for it is customary with them, when they make long journies, to use only one. They universally have the hind wheels higher than the fore wheels. There are some covered in their country manner, which are very handsome, and so light that, including wheels, it seemed that a man could carry one of them suspended to his neck. As the country is perfectly smooth and level, there is nothing to prevent the horse from being always on the trot. It is from this great evenness of the ground that when they plough they draw furrows of an extraordinary length.

Until I came to Pest, I had no servant; but there I treated myself with one, and took one of those french masons into my service whom I found at Pest: he was from Brai sur Somme.

On my return to Buda, I accompanied the milanese ambassador to pay our compliments to the grand count of Hungary, a title which answers to that of lieutenant of the emperor. The grand count received me with much distinction, because from my dress he took me for a Turk; but when he learnt I was a Christian, he was somewhat colder. I was told that he was a man whose conversation was little to be depended on, and that no great trust must be placed in his promises. This is somewhat generally the reproach made to the Hungarians; and for my part, I own, that after the idea given me of them by my acquaintance, I should have less confidence in an Hungarian than in a Turk.

The grand count is an old man. It was he, as I heard, who formerly arrested Sigismond king of Bohemia and Hungary, and afterward emperor, and threw him into prison, whence he afterwards released him by an amicable agreement.

His son was just married to a beautiful hungarian lady. I saw him at a tournament after their manner, when the combatants were mounted on small horses and low saddles: they were gallantly dressed, and had strong and short lances. It was a pleasing spectacle. Whenever the two champions hit, both perhaps, but certainly one of them must be unhorsed,— and it is then seen who has the firmest seat*.

When they tilt for golden wands, all the horses are of the same size, all the saddles of the same form,—and they are drawn for by lot, and the justers are taken by pairs: should one of two adversaries fall, the victor is obliged to retire, and is not permitted to tilt again.

* The knights in France were mounted for tournaments or battle on large strong horses called 'Palefrois.' Their saddles were high piqued before and behind, which afforded them greater means of resisting the shock of the lance than the small horses and low saddles of the Hungarians; and this is the reason our author says, that in the tilts of the Hungarians it may be easily seen which knight has the best seat on his horse.

I had never quitted the company of the milanese ambassador until we came to Buda; but he had told me on the road, that we must there separate, that he might continue his route to Milan. Soon after my return to Buda, I called, in consequence, on Clays Davion, who gave me a letter of recommendation to a merchant of his acquaintance at Vienna.

As I had fully opened myself to him, not thinking it right to make a secret of my rank, my name, or the country I had come from, or the honour I had of belonging to my lord duke of Burgundy, he had inserted all this in his letter, and I profited from it.

From Buda, I came to Thiat, a country town where the king is said to be fond of residing,—then to Janiz, in German ' Jane *,' a town on the Danube. I afterward passed by another town built on an island in that river, which had been given by the emperor to one of the dependants of the duke of Burgundy, whom I believe to be sir Renier Pot. I also

Jane. Q. Gen.

passed through Brut*, situated on a river that divides the kingdom of Hungary from the duchy of Austria. The river runs through a marsh, where a long and narrow causeway has been constructed. This is an important place, and I am convinced that a small body of men could effectually defend it on the austrian side.

Two leagues further the ambassador took leave of me, and followed another road to return to the duke of Milan, his lord. I took that leading to Vienna, where I arrived after five days journey.

On my entering the town, no one would lodge me, supposing I was a Turk. At last, by accident some one pointed out to me an inn where I was received. Fortunately my servant whom I had hired at Pest knew the hungarian and high german languages: he desired that the merchant to whom I had a letter might be sent for. On seeking him, he came, and not only offered me every service in his power, but went to

* Q. Bruck.

inform my lord duke Albert*, cousin-german to my lord, of my arrival, who instantly dispatched to me a poursuivant at arms, and shortly after sir Albrech de Potadorf.

Not two hours after my arrival, I saw sir Albrech dismount at the gate of my inn, and, hearing him ask for me, I thought myself undone. A little before my departure for the holy land I, with some others, had arrested him between Flanders and Brabant, because we thought him a subject of Frederick of Austria †, who had challenged my lord; and I now doubted not but that he was come in his turn to arrest me, and perhaps do worse.

He told me that his lord, duke Albert, having learnt that I was attached to the duke of Burgundy, had sent him to me to offer, on his part, every service that was in his power; that

* Albert II. duke of Austria, emperor after the death of Sigismond.

† Frederick duke of Austria succeeded Albert II. as emperor.

he defired me to ask whatever I might want as boldly from him as from my own lord, for that he wished to treat his servants in the same manner as he would his own. Sir Albrech then spoke for himself: he presented me with money, and offered me horses or any thing else; in short, he rendered me good for evil, although, after all, I had not done any thing to him but what honour permitted, and even ordered me to do.

Two days after, duke Albert sent to say he wished to speak with me; and sir Albrech again came to conduct me to him. I presented myself to him the moment he came from mass, attended by eight or ten old knights of a respectable appearance. Scarcely had I made my reverence, when he took me by the hand, and would not suffer me to speak to him on my knees. He asked many questions, particularly about my lord, which induced me to think he had a great affection for him.

He was of a tolerably good size, brown complexion, good humoured, affable, valiant and generous, and was said to possess every good quality. Among the persons who accompanied him were some lords from Bohemia, whom the Hussites had expelled from that country because they would not be of their religion.

At the same time, a great lord of that country, called Paanepot, was presented to him, who had come with several others, on the part of the Hussites, to treat with him, and establish peace.

These last proposed to march to the assistance of the king of Poland, against the lords of Prussia, and made, as I heard, great offers to duke Albert, if he would second them; but he replied, according to my information, that, until they submitted themselves to the religion of JESUS CHRIST, he would never make truce nor peace with them as long as he should live.

In fact, at this very time he had twice beaten them in battle; had conquered from them all Moravia; and, by his conduct and

valour, had aggrandized himself at their expense.
———On quitting his presence, I was conducted to that of the duchess, a tall handsome woman, daughter to the emperor, and heiress, after him, to the kingdoms of Hungary and Bohemia, and their dependancies. She had just been brought to bed of a daughter, which had occasioned festivals and tournaments, that were the more numerously attended, because, hitherto, she had not had any children.

On the morrow, the duke sent sir Albrech to invite me to dinner, and made me sit at his table with an hungarian lord and another, an Austrian. All his attendants are on board wages, and no one dines with him unless invited by the master of his household.

The table was square; and the custom is for one dish to be brought at a time, and for him who is nearest to eat of it, which supplies the place of a taster*. Fish and flesh were served,

---

* Formerly there was, at the tables of sovereigns, an officer to taste every dish before it was put on the table This precaution had originally been taken against poison.

and above all a quantity of meat strongly seasoned, but always dish by dish.

After the dinner, I was carried to see the dancing in the apartments of the duchess. She gave me a bonnet of gold thread and silk, a ring, and a diamond to wear on my head, according to the fashion of the country.

There were present many nobles of each sex,—and I saw there some very handsome women, with the finest heads of hair that can be conceived.

When I had remained in these apartments some time, a gentleman named Payser, who, though but a squire, was a chamberlain and keeper of the jewels of the duke of Austria, came, by his orders, to shew them to me. I saw the crown of Bohemia, which has some very fine diamonds, and the largest ruby I ever saw. It seemed bigger than a full-sized date; but it is not clear, and there are some cavities toward the bottom that shew a few black spots. ——The keeper then carried me to see the wague-bonnes*, which the duke of Austria had constructed to combat the Bohemians. I perceived none that could hold more than twenty men; but he assured me there was one that would contain three hundred, and did not require more than eighteen horses to draw it.

I met at this court the lord de Valse, a gallant knight, and the greatest baron in Austria after the duke. I saw there also sir Jacques Trousset, a handsome swabian knight; but there was another, named le Chant, hereditary cup-bearer to the emperor, who having lost his brother and many friends at the battle of Bar, and hearing that I belonged to my lord of Burgundy, caused me to be watched to know the day of my departure, that he might seize me as I was travelling through Bavaria. Luckily for me, the duke of Austria was informed of his intentions, and sent him away, making me stay longer at Vienna than I intended, to wait for the

* Waguebonne—is a sort of waggon, or moveable tower, used in war.

departure of the lord de Valse and sir Jacques Trousset, that I might accompany them.

During my stay, I witnessed three of the tournaments I mentioned, with small horses and low saddles. One took place at court,—the others in the streets; but at the last, several were unhorsed so heavily that they were dangerously wounded.

The duke of Austria made me in private offers of money. I received similar offers from sir Albert and sir Robert Daurestoff, a great lord in Austria, who, the preceding year, had travelled in disguise through Flanders, and had there seen my lord duke, and spoke very handsomely of him. In short, I received very pressing ones from a poursuivant of lower Brittany, named Toutseul, who, after having served under the admiral of Spain, was now in the service of the duke of Austria. This Breton called on me every day to go to mass, and attended me wherever I wished to go. Persuaded that I must have expended on my journey all the money I had, a little before my departure, he presented me with the value of fifty marcs in enamels, and insisted that I should sell them for my profit; but, as I equally refused to accept them or to borrow, he protested that no one should ever know any thing of it.

Vienna is a tolerably large town, well inclosed with deep ditches and high walls, inhabited by rich merchants and all sorts of tradesmen. The Danube washes its wall on the north side. The surrounding country is pleasant and good; and it is a place of amusement and pleasure. The natives are better dressed than those of Hungary, although they all wear coarse doublets, very thick and wide. In war they cover the doublet with an haubergeon, a glaçon*, a large hat of iron, and other armour usual in that country. They have many crennequiniers, for such is

---

* Glaçon or Glachon,—a kind of defensive armour. The French called ' Glaçon' a sort of fine cloth that was doubtless glazed. I suspect that glaçon in German was a kind of coat-armour made of many folds of quilted cloth, such as our gambisons. Perhaps it may be only a cuirasse.

the name given in Austria and Bohemia to those called archers in hungary. Their bows are like those of the Turks, but not so good nor so strong; and they do not use them so well as they do. The Hungarians pull the string with three fingers, and the Turks with the thumb and ring.

When I went to take leave of the duke and duchess of Austria, he recommended me himself to my two travelling companions, sir Jacques Trousset and the lord de Valse, who was setting off for his command on the frontiers of Bohemia. He repeated his question, as to my wanting money; but I answered, as I had before done to all who had offered me some, that my lord of Burgundy had so amply supplied me on my departure, that I had a sufficiency for my return to him, but that I requested he would grant me a safe conduct, which he did.

The Danube, for three days journey on leaving Vienna, runs eastward: from above Buda to the point of Belgrade, it takes a southerly direction, and then, between Hungary and Bulgaria, it resumes its easterly course, and falls, as they say, into the Black Sea at Mont Castre.

I left Vienna in company with the before mentioned lord of Valse and sir James Trousset. The first was going to his lady at Lintz, and the second to his country-seat.

After two days travelling, we came to Saint Polten, where the best knives of the country are made. Thence to Molke on the Danube, where is the best manufacture of cross-bows,—having beside a very handsome carthusian monastery. Thence to Valse, which belongs to the aforesaid lord. The castle is constructed on an elevated rock, that commands the Danube. He himself shewed me the ornaments of the altar of the chapel: I never before saw any so rich in embroidery and in pearls. I there also noticed boats drawn up the Danube by horses.

The morrow of our arrival, a bavarian gentleman came to pay his respects to the lord of Valse. Sir Jacques Trousset, informed of his arrival, declared he would hang him on a thorn in a garden. The lord de Valse hastened to him, and entreated he would not put such an affront on him in his own house. 'Well,' replied sir Jacques, 'should he come elsewhere within my reach, he shall not escape hanging.' The lord de Valse went to the gentleman, and made him a sign to go away, which he complied with. The cause of this anger of sir Jacques was, that he himself and the greater part of his attendants were of the secret company, and that the gentleman, having been also a member, had misbehaved *.

From Valse we came to Ens, situated on the river Ems;—thence to Evresperch, on the same river, and within the domain of the bishop of Passau,—and then to Lintz, a very good town, with a castle on the Danube, and not

* This relates, probably, to the famous secret tribunal; and the Bavarian, whom Trousset wanted to hang, may have been a false brother, who had revealed the secrets of it.

far from the frontiers of Bohemia. It belongs to the duke of Austria, and the lord of Valse is governor of it.

I saw there madame de Valse, a very handsome lady from Bohemia, who gave me a flattering reception. She presented me with an excellent trotter for the road, a diamond to put in my hair, after the austrian fashion, and a bonnet of pearls ornamented with a ring and a ruby *.

The lord of Valse remaining at Lintz with his lady, I continued my journey in company with sir Jacques Trousset, to Erfurt, which belongs to the count de Chambourg. Here Austria ends, and it had taken us six days to come from Vienna hither. From Erfurt we came to Riet, a bavarian town belonging to duke Henry,—then to Prenne on the river Sceine—to Bourchaze, a town with a castle on the same river, where we met the duke.—

* These bonnets must not be mistaken for such as ours. They were only wreaths, or circular crowns.

Thence to Mouldrof, where we crossed the Taing. In short, having traversed the country of duke Louis of Bavaria, without entering any of its towns, we arrived at Munich, the prettiest little town I ever saw, and which belongs to duke William of Bavaria.

I quitted Bavaria at Lansperch to enter Swabia, and passed through Mindelheim, that belongs to the duke, through Memingen, an imperial town, and thence to Walpourch, one of sir James's castles. He did not arrive until three days after me, because he had some friends to visit in the neighbourhood; but he had given orders to his people to treat me as they would do himself.

On his return, we set out for Ravensburg, an imperial town,—and thence to Martof, and Mersbourg, a town of the bishop of Constance seated on the lake of this name. The lake in this part may be about three italian miles broad. I crossed it and came to Constance, where I passed the Rhine, which there first assumes this name on issuing from the lake.

It was at this town that sir Jacques Trousset left me. This knight, one of the most amiable and valiant in Germany, had done me the honour and pleasure of accompanying me so far from respect to the duke of Austria, and would have escorted me further had he not been engaged at a tournament; but he gave me, in his stead, a poursuivant, whom he charged to escort me as far as I should wish.

This tournament had been undertaken by the lord de Valse. They loved each other like brothers, and were to tilt with war lances, bucklers and helmets of iron, according to the custom of the country, thirteen against thirteen, all friends and relations. Sir James was well furnished with every sort of arms, which he had shewn me himself in his castle of Walporch. I took my leave of him, and quitted him with much regret.

From Constance I went to Stein, where I crossed the Rhine,—thence to Shaffhousen, a town belonging to the emperor—to Waldshutts, to Lauffembourg, to Rhinfeld, all the property of duke Frederick of Austria—and to Basil, another imperial town, whither, on account of the council then assembled there, the emperor had sent duke William of Bavaria, as his lieutenant.

The duke and duchess were desirous to see me. I assisted at a session of the council, where he represented the emperor,—and among the numbers were the lord cardinal of St Angelo, legate from the holy father pope Eugenius, seven other cardinals, many patriarchs, archbishops and bishops. I met there several on the part of my lord of Burgundy, among whom were sir Guillebert de Lannoy, lord of Villerval, his ambassador, master Jean Germain and the bishop of Châlons. I had a conversation with the legate, who inquired much about the countries I had seen, especially Turkey. He seemed to have the conquest of this last much at heart, and recommended it to me to repeat to my lord of Burgundy certain particulars that I had told to him relative to such conquest.

At Basil I parted with my poursuivant, who returned to Austria; and having travelled through the country of Ferette, belonging to duke Frederick of Austria, and passed by Montbeliart, which is the property of the countess of that name, I entered Franche Comté, which belongs to my lord duke, and arrived at Besançon. I supposed that he was in Flanders, and consequently travelled on the frontiers of Bar and Lorraine to Veson; but at Villeneuve I learnt that he was on the frontier of Burgundy, and had caused Mussi l'Evêque to be besieged. I went then by Auxonne to Dijon, where I found the lord chancellor of Burgundy, in whose company I went to pay my respects to the duke. His people were at the siege, and he himself at the abbey of Poitiers.

I appeared in his presence dressed in the same manner as when I left Damascus, and had the horse led before him which I had purchased in that town, and which had brought me to France. My lord received me with much kindness. I presented to him my horse, my dress, with the Koran, and Life of Mohammed, written in Latin, which the chaplain to the venetian consul at Damascus had given me. He had these books delivered to master John Germain to examine: but I have never heard one word concerning them since that time. This master John was a doctor of divinity: he was bishop of Châlons-sur-Soane, and knight of the golden fleece *.

* Jean Germain, born at Cluni, and consequently a subject to the duke of Burgundy, had, when a child, pleased the duchess, who sent him to study at the university of Paris, where he distinguished himself. The duke, whose favour he afterward gained, made him, in 1431, *chancellor* of his order of the golden fleece, and not *knight*, as la Brocquière says. The year following he was nominated bishop of Nevers; sent in 1432 ambassador, first to Rome, and then to the council at Basil, as one of his representatives. In 1436 he was translated from the see of Nevers to that of Châlons-sur-Soane.

If I have said little respecting the country between this place and Vienna, it has been because it is well known. With regard to the others I have travelled through, I inform my readers, that the journey was not undertaken through ostentation or vanity, but for the guidance and information of such persons as may have similar desires as I have had to see and be acquainted with these countries, and in obedience to my highly redoubted lord the duke of Burgundy, who commanded me to write these travels. I always carried with me a small book, in which I wrote down my adventures whenever time permitted; and it is

What la Brocquière says of this bishop seems peevish; but if my readers will consider, that not hearing any thing of the two interesting manuscripts he had brought from Asia, there was cause for his being out of humour. Germain, however, was employed on them, but he was labouring to refute them. At his death, in 1461, he left two works in manuscript, copies of which are to be found in some libraries; one entitled, ' De Conceptione beatæ Mariæ Virginis, adversus Mahometanos et Infideles, Libri duo :' the other, ' Adversus Alcoranum, Libri quinque.'

from these memorandums that I have composed the history of my journey. If it be not so well composed as others could have done it, I must beg my readers to excuse me.

THE END.